TIMELESS TREASURES

Glen Connors

Copyright 2020 by Glen Connors

Published 2020.

Printed in the United States of America.

All rights reserved.

No portion of this book may be reproduced, stored in a retrieval system, or transmitted in any form or by any means – electronic, mechanical, photocopy, recording, scanning, or other – except for brief quotations in critical reviews or articles, without the prior written permission of the author.

ISBN 978-1-950647-39-2

Golden Strings Publishing

Publishing assistance by BookCrafters, Parker, Colorado.
www.bookcrafters.net

Table of Contents

Introduction...1
Chapter 1 Troubled Beginnings..................................5
Chapter 2 The Baby and the Burden.........................9
Chapter 3 The Doors of Discouragement..................12
Chapter 4 Heavenly Rescue......................................16
Chapter 5 Grandma's God...21
Chapter 6 My Quest for God.....................................31
Chapter 7 Grace Instead of Race..............................39
Chapter 8 Devastated Love.......................................48
Chapter 9 The Getaway...52
Chapter 10 Matrimony In the Making........................54
Chapter 11 The Unselfish Hero..................................60
Chapter 12 The Stranger Who Was Sorry.................66
Chapter 13 The Tornado and The Twig.....................70
Chapter 14 Fame, The Devils Spotlight.....................76
Chapter 15 The Wreck and The Resurrection...........82
Chapter 16 Purification and the Power to Preach.....93
Chapter 17 New York, Demons, and the Occult......108
Chapter 18 The Reunion of Reunions......................116
Chapter 19 The Dreamer..129
Chapter 20 The Revival That Broke Physical and
    Spiritual Deafness...137
Chapter 21 The Miracle Moving Hand of God.........147
Chapter 22 The Gift of Contentment to My Life,
    My Wife..162
Epilogue My Final Home..166

INTRODUCTION

The Lord God hath given me the tongue of the learned that I should know how to speak a word in season to him that is weary: He wakeneth morning by morning, He weakeneth mine ear to hear as the learned.
Isaiah 50:4

I WOULD LIKE TO BEGIN by telling you why I decided to write this book. God woke me out of my sleep at two o'clock on a Saturday morning on the fourteenth day of January, 1998. I heard a voice within me say, "Write a book about your life."

First I began to question it and wonder if it was the Lord or not, then I began to complain. I said, "Lord, you know it takes a long time to write a book and it's hard, I just don't have the time." So I closed my eyes and laid my head back down on the pillow. As I did, my inner man began to struggle with me and I couldn't sleep. I heard it again, "write a book about your life." Then I sat up on the side of the bed and heard a voice I knew was from God. God said, "When you write the book, I will help you and bring back to your memory the things you should write." Then He said, "I want you to title it "Timeless

Treasures." What did He mean by that? Instantly I knew what the title meant and I could see these little headings in my mind, each one was like the title of a chapter.

I believe each person on this earth who has ever come to Jesus has some special times in their lives they have never forgotten, times embedded in their memories for as long as they live. Those are the times God uses to change their lives. Some are hard times and some are good times but they are planted in your memory forever. As long as time shall last, those will still exist and become timeless. Those things that happened and changed our lives are really great treasures, things we can remember, share and use as testimonies. They become treasures to God also.

You know, a lot of events have happened in my life that I want to share with you, those timeless treasures God used to change my life.

I would also like to say, if this book is your hands, there is a reason. I have earnestly prayed for all who will read this book God told me to write, that there will be something in it causing you to remember a time in your life that will become a timeless treasure to you. I pray God will be able to use that treasure as a testimony to glorify God.

I know there are a lot of things written today that make you question if what you've heard or read is true or not. I would like to personally say to you, every word written in this book is true and I pray God confirms it to you.

*My heart is inditing a good matter:
I speak of the things
which I have made touching the king:
my tongue is the pen of a ready writer.*
Psalms 45:1

Chapter 1

TROUBLED BEGINNINGS

*I will be glad and rejoice in thy mercy:
for thou hast considered my trouble;
thou hast known my soul in adversities.*
Psalms 31:7

I WOULD LIKE TO START by telling you a little bit about my heritage; my mother and father. First of all, I was not raised by my mother and father but by another family who had taken me in. Therefore the information I am giving you about my mother and father are things told to me by them and others.

When I began to hear all they had to say about my life as a child during those years, I realized something I never knew. I was amazed that even before I was born, the devil had tried to destroy me. I know this one thing; the mighty, wonderful, guiding, protecting hand of God was there taking care of me and I thank Him for that today.

First I'll tell you about my mother; Freda Johnson, who was raised in Louisville, Kentucky. She knew the city life well, that is all she had known. When she was old enough to go to work in the city, one of the first jobs she had was in an ice cream shop where she met lots of friends. This was at a time when she was trying to decide what to do with her life.

One day a young man came into the ice cream shop whose name is Ralph Rasdall. The way she put it, "When I saw him, I knew I was in love." This nice young man caused her to forget about everything in life but him and they spent much time together getting to know each other. The more time they were together the more they wanted to be together. Ralph was not from the city but was raised in the country. They were literally brought up in two different environments but they still loved each other.

My mothers' family did not want her seeing this young man because they had heard things about him; how he drank and was involved in things that were not good. They told her she should not see him but she would not listen to what anyone said. She thought he was a nice man who was good to her and she wanted to make her own decisions.

A few years later when she was old enough, she decided to marry Ralph. I found out when they got married, most of my mothers' family; her mother, sisters, brothers and a lot of her aunts and cousins treated her differently because she had married the man they warned her about. She said the first few years of their marriage was the most wonderful time of her entire life and they were so happy. My father; Ralph, was a factory worker who had little education and didn't make much money but they were very happy.

After a few years passed, Ralph started to drink and go out with his friends. My mother said she was left alone many nights and did not know what she should do. Things were not being taken care of at home as they needed to be, bills were unpaid and her life was coming apart.

She knew her family would remind her of what they had

told her about Ralph, so to prove them wrong, she stayed and did everything she could to keep their marriage from coming to an end. But the drinking got worse and she just couldn't handle it anymore. She had to decide what to do and said she realized she would have to leave.

During this time my mother had two children; Deborah, my older sister, and me. She knew we had to be provided for but did not know how because she was unemployed. Where would she go and how would she support herself and her two children?

The first thing she decided to do was try to get a job. If she did, then she could get out of this marriage and start her life over. She told me about the terrible struggle she had trying to find work and all she had gone through. I cannot imagine all those hurts and how she must have felt with two young children depending on her.

She told me a story I will never forget. When I was still in her womb, an illness came upon her and also amnesia. She did not know how she got it and couldn't remember anything. The doctor told her the amnesia is sometimes caused by the illness she had as well as potential problems in an unborn child. This was true for me and I became clinically blind in one eye. When it came time for my mother to give birth, she realized the doctors knew something was wrong with my eye. They did everything they knew to do but nothing helped.

When I heard that, there was no question in my mind that somehow Satan knew God had a plan for me. At my birth, I don't know if angels were there and knew I would be attacked in some way or not, but God watched over me and protected me.

My mother told me something I will never forget. At that time she was not a person who went to church, never talked about knowing Jesus or having a relationship with Him. When they brought me into the delivery room, laid me in her arms for the first time, she looked upon my face and said there was a quiet stillness that came within her. She heard something say to her, "This child will be a minister, a minister for God." she said that was very strange and had never experienced anything like that before. You see, she never went to church and there was no member of our family she knew of who was a minister.

She never told anyone about that for almost thirty-five years until the day I found her then she revealed it to me. There was a reason for that and I will talk about that later. In later years she got involved in alcohol and a lot of things happened in her life she was ashamed of.

Satan did attack me as a child but God was still doing supernatural things to make sure I was cared for. I thank Him and praise Him so much for that. My mother and father were married at this time but she decided she wanted a divorce and was looking for work. She began to realize she could not take care of her two children and was so troubled, hurt and full of distress she did not know what step to take next.

The Lord also will be a refuge for the oppressed, a refuge in times of trouble.
Psalms 9:9

Chapter 2

THE BABY AND THE BURDENS

Come unto me, all ye that labour and are heavy laden and I will give you rest.
Matthew 11:28

MY MOTHER HAD MADE THE DECISION to divorce my father and look for work. She worked at some grocery stores and whatever else she could find to do. She told me that she, my sister and me lived in an apartment in Louisville, Kentucky. At that time I was about four years old and my sister was a few years older than me. Mother was getting very discouraged because the wages from her jobs were not enough to pay all of the bills.

She started going to bars, thinking she would meet someone there and wouldn't be so lonely. My mother was a talented and very good tap dancer. One of the bars offered her good money to tap dance there and she thought this was a wonderful opportunity. This was the first time she had made enough money to provide all the things we needed.

When my mother worked, my sister and I were left with Helen, a wonderful lady who lived next door. She was a woman with a heart full of love who attended a Catholic Church and loved my sister so much she wanted to raise her. Helen knew this was not the kind of life we should have. But of course, mother would not agree to that, so Helen just kept babysitting us.

My mother continued working at the bar but her conscience got to the place that she realized this wasn't the kind of life her children needed. But now she too was involved in drinking and with the men in a way she shouldn't be and started going home with different men. Her life was filled with such guilt and she worried about what was going to happen to her children. She told me she decided to leave my sister with Helen and let her keep her for a while. She knew it was too much for Helen to keep both of us so she wanted to take me back to some members of her family. She thought if she had to leave me, she wanted me to be with her family.

I will never forget the tears in her eyes when she told me the things she experienced. After leaving my sister with Helen she continued her job working in the bar, but she wanted to leave and do something better with her life to prevent her children from being raised in that kind of life and environment. Her children were such a burden on her at that time; because of her lifestyle, she said every time she looked at us she thought "What if they become what I am? I have to change my life."

Nothing better came along, nothing seemed to work out. She never went to church, never brought it to God and was still struggling with life, trying to handle it herself with all that she had. She thought there would be something she could do, some ability she had to handle it.

I'm sure all of us have come to that place believing we can handle life on our own. But you know God seems to always bring us to a place that makes us realize we cannot handle everything in life and we ***do*** need the Lord.

Humble yourselves therefore under the mighty hand of God that he may exalt you in due time. (7) Casting all your care upon him, for he careth for you.
1 Peter 5:6-7

Chapter 3

THE DOORS OF DISCOURAGEMENT

Can a woman forget her sucking child, that she should not have compassion on the son of her womb? Yea, they may forget, yet will I not forget thee.
Isaiah 50:15

THIS IS PROBABLY one of the most touching events of my life told to me by my mother that I seem to never forget. Mother told me that now, me being a little boy of four years old, she realized she had to do something with her life or do something with her children.

She decided to go back to the members of her family and tell them she wanted to leave me with the family until she could afford to do something better. She would try to get a better job, work on her life, and then come back to get her children. I have never forgotten the expression on her face and how hard it was for her to say the words as she told me the story.

She began going to members of her family, one by one talking to them, asking if they could take care of me until she was better able to. One door after another was shut and every one she asked to keep me said no, it was just too much of a burden to take in this four year old child. Her family reminded her constantly she should have never been with the man they had warned her of.

I thought to myself, Oh, my God, how many of us have been guilty of looking at somebody's life because of what they have done and began to run them down, not knowing we have no right to judge. We do not know their hearts, we do not know when they want to change or when God wants to do something wonderful and glorious with them. The things that we say to them can be the very reason they become what they are. Their life can be crushed by our condemnation, while thinking we are doing something good. God help us if we do that.

One door after another was shut. I don't know how my mother felt, but she continued going because she thought someone would eventually help so that I would not be left away from the family.

For several weeks she continued to go but no one would help. That is why I call this chapter "The Doors of Discouragement." She became so discouraged at that time, she really wanted to give up on life itself, even thinking about suicide. The only thing that kept her from following through with it was when she would look at me, at my little face, she would realize something needed to be done for me.

My mother continued to dance at the bar but every free moment she had, she put in applications for a better job; nothing came along. She stopped putting in applications and decided to make this her profession, even if it killed her. Whatever happened, she needed to find somewhere for me.

A country musician, Romer, came into the bar where my mother worked. They began to talk and get to know one another. His band played at the same bar and they became close friends. She told Romer about her little boy and how worried she was not knowing what to do.

"I know something you can do," Romer told her. "My sister cannot have children and wants a child so bad, she would give anything if she could find a little boy and raise him. I will take him in my home and care for him while you are trying to look for work. I am willing to keep him for a little while and if you don't come for him, I will take him to my sister. She will take care of him and not charge you anything, you will have someone to keep your child for a little while. If you decide to let him go, I know she will want to take him."

My mother said she didn't know whether to be happy or sad, but thought it was her only way out. Romer took me and called his sister telling her about me. Of course she was so excited she did not know what to do. I was in a strange place with strangers and all I could think was, where is my mother? All of the doors had been shut. Have you ever felt like that in life? That all the doors have been shut? The Bible tells us that Jesus said, "I am the door." I wish my mother could have understood it at that time and went to that Door. I know God had a plan where she could have kept me, she just did not know.

Friend, there are many people in the world today who just don't know. You and I, as Christians, need to let them know. If you have an experience in your life that can help someone, share it. We can all learn from each other's mistakes. I am so thankful that at least my mother was concerned enough and loved me enough to be sure I was going to be taken care of. Romer said the clothes I had on were very ragged, that I was very skinny looking like I had not been eating very well and that I wasn't very clean. They took me and tried to clean me up, feed me some good food and got me some better clothes.

You know, when I think of that story, it just comes to my

attention, and I believe God is that same way. God is looking down from heaven at all the people who have been hurt by the system; the devil's system, and wrecked their lives. God wants to feed them, clothe them and help them because they are His children.

> *When saw we thee a stranger and took thee in? or naked and clothed thee? (39) Or when we saw thee sick, or in prison and came unto thee (40) And the King shall answer and say unto them, verily I say unto you inasmuch as ye have done it unto one of the least of these my bretheren, ye have done it unto me.*
> Matthew 25:38-40

Chapter 4

HEAVENLY RESCUE

Favour is deceitful, and beauty is vain,
but a woman that feareth the Lord, she shall be
praised. (31) Give her of the fruit of her hands;
and let her own works praise her in the gates.
Proverbs 31:30-31

PRAISE GOD, it's about time something good is going to happen. Now Romer decides to take me to his sister; Lillie, and I remember him telling me the first time she saw me, she literally broke down in tears. She had been praying to God for a child because she wanted a child so bad but could not have one. She did not think they could adopt a child because they had little money. She did not know of any way to adopt so she took it to God. When she looked at me, she just knew I was the little boy God was going to give her.

Let me tell you some things about this incredible lady. She probably did not stand much over five feet tall but had a heart as tall as the Empire State Building. Even though she did not have a lot of money, she was willing to give everything she had to anyone who needed it. Lillie lived in an environment full of pain, distress and hurt but was a prayer warrior who knew how to talk to God. Oh yes, she was little in stature, but she was not little in the eyes of God.

Yes, God had sent me just what I needed; friends, it was a heavenly rescue. I would like to tell you about my life as a child with this family, about my Christian mother I now had and my alcoholic father; Wilbur, who loved me so much but was so misunderstood. He was Lillie's husband and he worked on tractor trailers in Louisville, Kentucky. He was a hardworking man who was also very knowledgeable about nature.

We lived in Edmondson County, Kentucky. Green River runs through it and Mammoth Cave is also there. Some of the greatest wooded parts of Kentucky are in this area so there is much wildlife. People came from all over the country to ask Wilbur about fishing spots, trapping and his knowledge of the woods. But there was something in Wilbur's life that was not good. Yes, he too was involved in alcohol and once again I have ended up back in that environment.

Wilbur loved me so much, it seemed I was the only thing in his life that had any value. He treated me as good as he knew how, being who he was. Everyone around us, even the church people, talked about Wilbur because he was an alcoholic. Wilbur wanted to know God and I believe somehow, in his heart, he did. He had such a terrible time trying to get out of the world of alcohol, it was beginning to consume him, to destroy his life. I came right in the middle of his struggles.

When he was drinking, Wilbur was very violent to the people around him. Though he was never violent with me, he seemed to always be violent with Lillie, my new mother. In that kind of environment, we lived in a troubled situation all the time. Night after night we would have to get up and leave. We would stay all night with someone else because of all the trouble, fighting, arguing and the terrible things being said. There were many times when he would hit and injure her, even occasions when he loaded his gun and try to kill her. That was our life.

In the middle of all that, Lillie was a lady who would try to go to church, she wanted to serve Jesus. A minister had raised this little lady and whatever had gotten into her heart had never left her. She still respected what was right and remained in that troubled marriage for years and years. Later in life I asked her why she stayed so long and she said it was because she wanted me to have a home. My heart fell within me when she said that, thinking she went through many years of misery because she wanted me to have a place to stay. Yes, she might have been little in stature, but oh what a mighty woman she was in God. Things I experienced in this family literally changed my life as I was growing up.

Let me tell you what happened from the beginning. After Romer left me with Lillie and Wilbur, I remember one thing, I kept going to the front door. Every morning, I woke up and ran to the open front door with a locked screen door going to the porch. I ran to that screen door and looked out.

After Romer took me to Lillie's, Freda; my birth mother who had been dancing at the bars would come to that door and knock. She would visit me a little while and then have to leave. I was so excited when she came every morning that I always got up early and ran to that screen door to see if Mother was coming.

One day when she came over, she had a talk with Lillie. I remember her saying she would not be back for a long time. The next morning I got up and ran to the screen door as usual. I waited for hours but Mother did not come. I did that for several days, several weeks, and then finally realized Mother was not coming back. Being only four years old, it was hard for me to understand, but finally I realized I needed to stop looking out that screen door. Lillie tried to do things to comfort me and get if off my mind.

    I will never forget, one of the first things she did was take me to the store and bought me two ice cream cones. I looked up at her and said, "Two ice cream cones for me? Both for me? Lillie said yes, they are both yours. She was amazed at my being so excited about getting two of something. This had never happened before. She bought me two pieces of gum then two pieces of candy. She wanted to buy me things in twos because it thrilled me so much. I was so amazed by this woman who would do that for me that I began to really love her.

    I began to grow and develop in life and soon reached my teen years. When I was a teenager, I found out there were some things I was talented at and some things I was not. One thing I was talented at was singing. When I was going to school and singing in the programs, I discovered they liked my singing. They put me in all the plays they had and the music teacher thought I had an excellent ability to sing. I also learned to play instruments and played them really well. I played the drums, guitar and began to play the piano some. I chose to stay with the guitar because I enjoyed it the most. Then as I got better on the guitar, I made up my mind, this is what I love so this is what I am going to do. I decided I wanted to be a star and as soon as I was of age, I was going to hit the road. The closest place I could do that was in Nashville, Tennessee. I was going to write some of the greatest songs written in the history of music, I was sure of it because I also had the ability to write songs.

    My mother had different plans though and wanted to take me to church to try to get my heart right with God first, but I didn't want to listen. I went to church but when I could get out of it, I didn't go. When I couldn't get out of going, I would just go to be with Mother, to satisfy her. She prayed earnestly for me, wanting me to get my life right with God. She was such a wonderful woman but my plans were totally different. God was the last thing in the world I had on my mind. All I thought about was the fun I could have as a teenager and being a professional musician one day. That is what my life was literally wrapped up in.

Oh, listen to me well, never, never underestimate the power of prayer, even from a little woman.

> *For we have not an high priest which cannot be touched with the feeling of our infirmities, but was in all points tempted like as we are, yet without sin. (16) Let us therefore come boldly unto the throne of grace that we may obtain mercy and find grace to help in time of need.*
> Hebrews 4:15-16

Chapter 5

GRANDMA'S GOD

Who can find a virtuous woman?
for her price is far above rubies.
Proverbs 31:10

I WOULD LIKE TO TELL YOU about my grandmother Ellie; Lillie's mother, and her husband; Elza Jaggers. He was a minister, a wonderful man and he preached the gospel in many revivals. Other ministers would come to his home and discuss the Word of God with him so I was around the Word of God a good deal of the time.

When Lillie went to work, I was left with Ellie and Elza. I lived about two miles from the school and liked walking to school rather than riding the bus in the summer. I walked right by Grandmother and Grandfather's house on the way home from school so I would stop and visit with them. I stayed with them if Mother wasn't going to be home and was with my grandparents more than anyone.

I want to tell you a few things about my grandfather. He did not live very long after I met him but I will never forget one thing about him as long as I live. Sometimes when he preached he would slap the back of his right hand with his left hand but he only did that when he really got excited, then you knew God was really going to move upon him. When Grandfather preached, he didn't care if he was dressed in a suit or not, one time he even wore "gum boots" that came up to his knees. He was a simple man who believed God's word and he stood for it.

They went to a little praying country church. It was not like any elaborate church of today. A lot of the men wore overalls and the women wore long dresses. There was a potbelly wood stove they used in the winter to heat the church.

He sometimes would have a message that was out of the ordinary and everyone knew it was God. He was a man who believed in getting to the place where you truly let God take over and you do or say what God wants you to in the Spirit. He preached a lot on shouting, for us not to be ashamed to shout with a voice of triumph to our God, to know whom we serve and never forget Him. He deserves to be worshiped and glorified.

Many times I heard my grandfather shout right in the middle of his message. I know we don't see or hear as much of this today as we need to. There is another thing I remember about Grandfather, he had a favorite song he liked to sing at the end of his messages, "I Want to Die A Shouting." When he sang that song it always made me cry. Sometimes he would sing it at the house when it was quiet and no one else was around. He would sit in his rocking chair singing and the words in that wonderful song touched my heart so much. I was only a teenager at the time, but it really and truly moved me.

My grandfather got very sick and eventually went into a coma. Grandmother did not want to keep him in the hospital and they were a large family who wanted to take care of him so they put a hospital bed in their home and Grandmother took care of him.

You have to realize, Grandfather had twelve children, although not all were living then. With such a large family when children and grandchildren were all there, they literally filled the house. They knew by the doctor's reports that Grandfather was going to die so they were coming over quite often and Grandmother was working overtime to take care of him. While the family was there they moved him to the couch, even though he was in a coma, so they could be there with him.

Grandfather lay in a coma for weeks not speaking a word, then an amazing thing happened. Grandfather slowly opened his eyes and said "I want to see Glen. Tell Glen to come here, I want to see Glen." One of the family members ran to the kitchen and told me, "Grandfather wants to see you." I said, "What?" They said again, "Grandfather is awake and he wants to see you."

I could hardly believe it so I ran to the living room where they had him on the couch and got down on one knee where I could get close and hold on to his hand. "Yes, Grandfather?" I said. He took his hand out of mine and placed it on my head and said "Son, you are a good boy. God is going to use you and bless you. I want you to stay away from the things that are wrong because God is going to use you and He is going to use you for Himself."

I didn't understand it then and had no idea what that meant. I knew nothing about God or what he was talking about at all. I did not know he literally was laying his hands on me and prophesying about my life, that God had a plan for me and he was passing an anointing on me. Right after my grandfather did that, tears came to my eyes. I remember looking at him and seeing the big smile on his face. After he said what he wanted to say to me, he shut his eyes and went back into the coma. Everyone was just amazed.

The whole room was changed. No one was talking anymore and they picked him up and put him back in his bed. Grandmother was crying, she thought God was healing him and he was coming out of the coma, but that was not the case. Although God did bring him back long enough to give me a message. I often wonder why Grandfather had *me* come in there. He had all these children and grandchildren, why *me*? I have never forgotten that about Grandfather. God had something on His mind planned for me.

When he began to get worse and could not be fed, they took him to the hospital. The doctors said it was just a matter of time and he couldn't last much longer. Grandmother had now become almost hysterical and many members of the family were coming by every day, being sure someone was always near if something should happen. I was there the day Grandfather passed away and God allowed me to witness what happened.

My grandfather was lying in the hospital bed with needles stuck in both arms with tubes running up to bottles that were putting fluids in his body. He was lying there helpless and seemed as if he had no life left in him. All of a sudden, out of nowhere, Grandfather sat up in his bed; straight up with the strength of someone like you or me, and with the back of his right hand that he used when he preached, he began to slap those hands together. He began to shout, a shout that only he could do when he said, "Hallelujah, praise the Lord and glory to God!" Anybody who had ever heard him preach knew this was his own personal shout God had given him. He shouted for a few minutes and seemed to be in no pain. There was something wonderful happening to Grandpa. Then he lay down and died.

The first thing I thought of was the testimony he lived was the testimony he died with and then his favorite song, "I Want to Die Shouting," with his hands slapping together just as when he preached. He left the world with the same testimony. God was with him and he could still shout with a voice of triumph, even in a coma.

That changed my life, touched my heart but also ripped it out. I knew being in that room was my first encounter of having a true experience with God. Grandfather was taken out of our lives and now when I came home from school, there was only Grandmother. A lot of times she would sit in the swing all alone and I could see the brokenness in her heart. She had such love for this man that most people in the world today have never experienced. She had a love that was faithful and true. He was the only man she wanted to love or ever would love, but she had someone with her who is greater, God himself.

I can never say enough about my grandmother. Many times I have thought about how I would sum up her life and what the right words would be to describe her. It's very simple, she was a "Word" woman. That's the best way I know how to say it, a Word woman. Her life was a life of nothing but the word of the living God. She didn't just talk it and know it, she lived it. She was left to be the impact on my life that would cause me to come to know God. That is why I titled this chapter "Grandma's God" because she definitely knew this God. Yes, this Grandmother who taught me about God had lost her husband and now, even with her great faith, she was so alone.

I felt sometimes that God had sent me to fill in the gap of her loneliness and at the same time she was doing the same for me. God knows the right time to send someone into our lives.

Sometimes it seems like it's going to be a burden but all the time it's going to be a blessing. You would think maybe at a time like that I would be a burden for her when she was the one who needed taken care of, but God used both of us, putting us together to help each other's hurts and loneliness.

There are so many good things I could say about my grandmother but it would fill a hundred books. I want to say it in a way you will understand just how much she meant to me my life.

My grandmother; who had taken care of me when my mother worked, who I stopped to see after school, now Grandmother had been by herself for several years. She always kept her house spotless but was now getting to the place where she could not take care of everything in her home so I came by to do things she needed done around the house, take her to the store, cut her wood and generally whatever she needed me to do. When I think of my grandmother, I think of the word "respect." I remember I never saw her dressed immodestly and never saw her knees in my life. She had hair that went nearly to the ground but she rolled it up and kept it in a bun. I'm not saying she was trying to be holy with her hair, but she was a woman dedicated in everything she did. She believed in holiness and what was right. If anybody said anything that was wrong according to the word of God, she immediately corrected them by saying, "But thus saith the Lord."

I want to tell you some things about my grandmother. First, she had a huge feather bed and when I went upstairs and fell down on it, my whole body just sank down in it. I loved that feather bed.

Sometimes my mother or other members of the family would come over and stay all night. I will never forget what

Grandmother would do around eleven o'clock when everyone was asleep. She put her robe on, wrap herself real well, walk up those steps and quietly say, "Glen, wake up." When I woke up she asked if I wanted something to eat, and of course I said yes. She knew I loved to eat but she also knew if the family saw me eat a lot all the time, they would think I was taking advantage of Grandmother, so she fixed me a small meal when anyone was there but put something back for me. Then when they were asleep, she woke me up and said, "Come on down. I have you something."

When I got down to the kitchen table, the food she put back just for me was sitting there. She would look at me, smile and say, "I love you, son." I will never forget that. It may seem like a little thing to you but it wasn't little to me. I remember the kind of love Grandmother had but there was something else I remember about her, one characteristic that changed my life. Not only was she filled with love but she was so unselfish, giving anything she had to help someone. She was the most praying woman I knew and I remember waking up sometimes at five o'clock in the morning; the sun had not come up, and I would hear her praying. Mostly she would be praying the word of God and she would pray for every child she had. She would be binding Spirits and praying protection over all her grandchildren.

There was one thing she always prayed that just shook me to the roots; she prayed for me to be saved. So many mornings I would wake up and hear that little voice cry out to God, "Oh, heavenly Father, would you save Glen? Heavenly Father, you have sent him here and he's been a blessing, but Father, would you save him? Would you change him? Would you make him see that he can't have a successful life without you, God?" When she prayed that prayer she didn't know I heard it and that it was doing something to me nothing else had ever done before. It was wonderful to know she cared for me this much.

That prayer changed my life and I remember running from God after hearing it. I was scared of God and afraid I was going to get saved. Then I wouldn't be able to be with my friends and do all the things I loved doing if I was going to try to be holy like that. I would literally run with everything in me. I tell you again friends, don't ever underestimate the power of prayer, not even prayers a little elderly woman prayed. You see, God is no respecter of persons when it comes to prayer. God heard those prayers she prayed and she lived to see them answered! I thank God for women who pray those kinds of prayers.

One day three large knots as big as an egg came up on my side. I have never been in that kind of pain in my entire life so they rushed me to the hospital. The doctors said I had an enlarged colon requiring surgery and there was no other way to treat it. Colon surgery is serious and it takes a long time to recover. Removing part of the colon would affect my digestive system for the rest of my life. My mother became hysterical, thinking I might die during surgery.

About ten o'clock one night, all my visitors had gone and I had been given so many drugs I hardly knew anything. Here comes Grandmother into my room carrying her little purse and a wrap around her shoulders. She took her hand brushing my hair back and kissed me on the forehead. "Glen," she said, "I'm here because God sent me." I looked at her and knew if she told me something like that, she was serious. "I am going to pray for you," she said. "Don't you worry, you are going to get well."

I was getting ready to face surgery the next morning and thought that was kind of ridiculous considering all the pain I was in. Grandmother got down on her knees beside the bed and began to pray. She raised her hand up then put it in mine. I have never heard such a prayer from that day to this. I know heaven shook when she began to pray that prayer and she took authority. It wasn't just a prayer that said heal this little boy or heal my grandson, she prayed a prayer that shook heaven with great authority and great power.

Later I found out that her church did not teach some of the things she did but she knew the word of God and that is what matters. She was not going to let the devil have me so she began to pray with authority and power to shake the heavens and plead the blood taking authority over evil spirits. As she prayed, there was a peace that came over me. Probably everyone on that floor of the hospital heard her raise her voice in prayer, but she just didn't care. When she got up, she brushed my hair back again, kissed my forehead, and whispered, "Sleep son, just sleep."

I got up the next morning and the first thing I remember was my side was not hurting and didn't understand why. I felt my side and realized the knots were gone, I just could not believe it. I could not even make my mind realize what had happened and kept pushing my side trying to figure out if the knots had moved or something, then it hit me! Could God have healed me? I pushed the button for the nurse and when she came in, I told her I knew she was supposed to prep me for surgery, but I didn't have any knots on my side and asked her to have the doctor see me first. God made it happen and the doctor stopped by, even though he wasn't supposed to be there at the time. He looked at me and said they would not be doing the surgery, just observe me.

They finally released me after a few days of no pain, no knots, and no discomfort at all. From that day until now, I have never had a problem with my colon. I had been away from home for several years years working and in that time God had dealt with my heart about preaching the gospel. I went back home and had a chance to see Grandmother. "Grandmother," I told her, "God has called me to preach the gospel." When she looked at me, I had never seen such a smile on her face. "You remember what I told you," she said as she looked at me. "What things so ever you desire, when you pray, believe that you shall receive them and you shall have them. I prayed that you would be a minister."

It shook me and grabbed me inside. I began to realize that what God was doing wasn't because I made up my mind what I wanted to do. God had already set it in motion through the prayers of His people and He had already prepared the way.

That was the last time I saw Grandmother. God has called her home but I know one day I will see her again in heaven where God has given her a reward for everything she did for me.

You know friend, this is something we can all learn from. You see, it is not who or what we are that causes great things to happen with God. It is a heart willing to reach out and do all we can, but only by believing in God's power working in us. This great lady taught me there is nothing impossible with God. She taught me about faith and many things I would never have learned had I not spent time with this woman who knew God. Yes, the perfect title for this chapter is, "Grandma's God."

Jesus said unto him, if thou canst believe all things are possible to him that believeth.
Mark 9:23

Chapter 6

MY QUEST FOR GOD

Behold, I stand at the door and knock: if any man hear my voice, and open the door, I will come in to him, and will sup with him, and he with me.
Revelation 3:20

NOW I HAD TO ASK myself a question. The God of Abraham, Isaac, Jacob, Moses, Elisha and the God of my grandmother, was He going to be just their God or was He also going to be my God?

This is how my life was turned over to God. When I was thirteen years old, there was a revival held at a little country church called Cove Hollow Baptist Church. Bob Vincent was the pastor holding the revival and my mother; Lillie, was attending the revival every night.

One day while I was at school, the Lord moved upon my mother and impressed on her heart she needed to pick me up because there was going to be some morning services at the revival and she wanted me there. This meant she needed to take off from work and take me out of school.

She drove over to the schoolhouse and asked for me to come

out of the classroom and talk to her in the hall. She looked at me with tears running down her cheeks and said, "Glen, would you go to church with me this morning? They are having revival services this morning. Would you go with me?"

She would never make me go, never force me but the first thing that came to my mind was, "Man, I can get out of school for an hour or two. Yes, I'll go." So I went with her to the meeting.

Bob Vincent went to the pulpit and preached his message titled, "There is no middle ground with God." He talked about how one day there was going to be a great tribulation, about how the heavens were going to be shaken and things were going to happen that would bring such fear upon men they would want to kill themselves. He talked about the moon turning to blood and the stars falling. He preached with great power and glory, and you know, it got hold of me about the way the heavens were literally going to be changed by God because He was trying to warn man.

When I heard that message I was so troubled I decided I wasn't going back to church. The next night Mother wanted me to go to the revival with her so I pretended to be sick. I did pretty well with that, and got away with it. She went on to the revival at church without me. I was lying on the bed and remember looking out my window at the sky and the moon. I kept hearing over and over in my mind the words of that minister saying the moon was going to turn to blood. I didn't know what that meant then but now I understand that it means the moon is going to turn blood red and the great and noble day of the Lord is coming. All I knew then was that God really was going to change the heavens.

The minister explained that God loved us so much He would do things, even change the heavens because He is trying to get our attention. I thought, my God, if there is a God, how could He love me that way? Then I thought, if it is true, that great tribulation is coming. I looked out the window seeing that moon and thought if it was to happen now, if Jesus Christ were to come today, I'm not ready, I know I'm not ready. I tried to turn over and go to sleep by covering my head. I know you will laugh at this but I even tried to take my mind off of it by talking to myself.

Have you ever done anything like that? I did, and you know what, it didn't work. The moon did not go away and the conviction did not go away. The moon kept reminding me of the message and the conviction in my heart kept reminding me that I was not right; I did not have God.

So I decided to get down at the side of my bed and pray. I had so much in my heart that I wanted to tell God but the only thing in the world I was interested in was that I needed to be saved. I was not really convinced there was a God. I wanted to know if He was real and I remember praying, "Lord, I know I am lost and don't have you. I know from the message the preacher preached that he really had an experience with You so if you are real God, I want you to reveal it to me. I don't want to just say it or just tell somebody I am saved, I want to know You are God. Please show me, please save me. I want to **know** it."

When I said those words, I will never forget what the Holy Spirit spoke to me. These words came from heaven to my inner being. "Arise, my son," (I loved that He called me His son.) "Arise and go to your father and tell him you are saved." That was probably one of the hardest things I had ever done. My father drinks and is not interested in church or God and for me to go in there and tell my drunken father that I was saved made no sense to me at all. The devil tried to fight me and said,

"If you go in there telling him you are saved, and you don't even know if you really **are** saved, what good is that going to do? It's going to embarrass you."

All at once it was like something supernatural began to help me and I began to pray again. I prayed, "O God, I will do what You said because now I believe You are God. But if I go in there and tell my father I am saved and You don't reveal it to me, I'll come back here and fall on my knees." I was going to find God one way or the other.

I went to the bedroom where my dad was usually lying drunk, or at least half drunk, and in no mood for anyone to talk to him. He was awake but not drunk, which was very rare. He didn't look like he had been drinking at all. I looked at him and realized this was God's timing so that my father would know what I did, that he would be aware of it. I reached out my hand and he grabbed it.

"Dad," I said. "The Lord has just saved me." When I said those words there was a presence of God that came upon me that brought a release. I knew what that scripture meant that says you become a new creature in Christ Jesus. If any man be in Christ he is a new creature.

I knew all of the resentment, fear, worry, doubt that He wasn't God and all of the sins in my life were now gone. I knew He saved me and there was such a presence of peace that came over me, I knew God was answering my prayer. He was revealing to me just what I prayed, showing me that He was God and He is real. I remember being happy and filled with so much joy as I walked through this narrow hallway to the living room. There were pictures on the wall and the glory of God was upon me so that the picture frames seemed to be glowing. I knew God was revealing to me what I had asked of Him.

I was so happy I shouted, I didn't shout once, if I shouted ten times, I shouted twenty times. If not twenty times, I shouted thirty times. I could not stop shouting. I raised my hands for the first time in my life and did a little dance up and down the hallway telling God how much I loved Him and thanked Him for saving my soul and just basking in His glory.

After it all ended, I realized, my God, I could not keep this to myself. I have to tell somebody so I got on the telephone and started calling my aunts and everybody I could think of, to tell them how God had saved my soul. What bothered me most was that most people I called didn't answer and I could hardly stand it. I thought, who am I going to tell, what am I going to do?

My mother came home from the revival about that time. We lived down in a valley and you had to go up over the hill to get out of the valley to the main highway. My aunt had been taking my mother to the revival and was bringing her back home. My mother was going to walk down from the top of the hill and I saw her standing up there so I thought as I ran out on the porch that I was going to scream out and tell her I was saved. But then I thought no, I'll just wait until she walks down the hill. Believe it or not, and this is the truth, as I looked up the hill at my mother, I could see God had done something to her, a presence on her that was such joy.

She was coming quickly down the hill and saw me. She said, "Oh! You're saved! You're saved! I couldn't believe it at first but then I thought that shouldn't be hard to believe because she had been praying for me for years. God had already revealed it to her. I went up to Mom and told her the Lord had saved me. And let me tell you friends, we got on shouting ground again. We had one spell after another, one tear after another. I ran up the hill to tell my aunt, who was in the car, what had happened to me. She looked at me and the spirit of the Lord came upon her and she began to prophecy to me and said, "You are the one God sent that He said He was going to send back out."

I didn't know what she meant at the time. But God was telling me I wasn't a blood member of their family but God had sent me there. Now He was going to send me back out to minister. I didn't know what any of that meant but my Aunt Leora knew exactly what it meant. I was filled with such joy I could not sleep all night and I knew from that moment on I was going to have to live for the Lord and put all of my heart into serving God. He was blessing me so much, it was probably the happiest time of my entire life.

About three years after that wonderful experience, another tragedy came my way. My mother and father, Lillie and Wilbur, had such a terrible time in their marriage because of his alcohol problem. We moved to Elizabethtown, Kentucky where my father had bought a mobile home and parked it in a mobile home park. We were having a hard time paying our bills because he was wasting money and we were about to lose our home. Mother didn't know what we were going to do. She was trying to work but it was not enough to pay all the bills. I knew I needed to go to work and help her or we were going to be out so I left school and landed a job at Burger King. I thought to myself, I have to do something to help Mother. She had done so much for me all my life and, education or no education I have to help her.

Mother didn't want me to quit school but I did. I couldn't stand to see her suffer. I earned only a very small check. I came home tired but I was young so it didn't bother me.

Something terrible happened one night. I walked down the dark alley to the mobile home park. When I got there I saw the base the mobile home sat on but it was gone. I thought I must have been seeing things wrong because I knew we lived at this location and I knew good and well that our home sat there. Maybe I'm looking at the wrong angle or something. Where is it? Then I realized it had been repossessed. I knew that Mother and Father had been having a lot of arguments lately and that she was becoming really scared of him. Of course my dad was drunk quite a bit and was threatening to kill my mother. Mother thought I was with him; he thought I was with her. They had both left, going separate ways. The trailer was gone and I was standing alone on the cement pad it had sat on. It was getting late and dark. As I looked around the park, I had only one friend there so I went over, knocked on the door and asked if they knew why the mobile home was gone. Of course they said they didn't know and since I did not know these people very well, I didn't want to stay there with them.

I was confused so I stayed around the park thinking someone would return. I waited as long as I could but I was becoming afraid and decided to walk to town where there would be people, then I wouldn't be out there alone. Before getting to town, I saw a barbershop across the street I had seen before but had never been inside. I had a little bit of money in my pocket and was thinking I needed a haircut so I went over there. Inside there were only black people. I was so troubled and hurt, not knowing what to do, I just wanted to go in somewhere and sit down and rest.

Little did I know God was getting ready to fulfill something in my heart I hadn't even dreamed! My quest for God, the heading for this chapter, yes I did find God and I was gloriously saved but now God was about to take me somewhere to show me things about Him I had never known.

It is marvelous how God can bring you to the places you need to be. You just seem to stumble into them, thinking it's some kind of coincidence when all the time God is guiding your steps. He had a master plan for my next destination and He was going to do some great things in the future. A wonderful thing happened to me at that barbershop. This was going to be one of the major turning points in my life while it seemed one of the most troubled times of my life. God has still used it so that He would get glory out of it. Not only that, it would change my life to the point that one day I would live for Him and do the things He chose for me to do because I came to this place and was with these people.

But we all, with open face beholding as in a glass the glory of the Lord, are changed into the same image from glory to glory, even as by the Spirit of the Lord.
2 Corinthians 3:18

Chapter 7

GRACE INSTEAD OF RACE

*Then Peter opened his mouth, and said Of a truth
I perceive that God is no respecter of persons:
(35) But in every nation he that feareth Him, and
worketh righteousness, is accepted with Him.*
Acts 10:34-35

THIS IS AN AMAZING STORY I am going to tell you. I assure you every word is true. When I went into that barbershop and sat down, I looked around and it was true, every person there was a black person. The barber was also black. I was sitting over in the corner in a chair by myself and was so hurt that I could not keep from holding my head down, almost in my lap. I was shaking inside and trying every way in the world to keep it from showing.

The barber's name was Dixon who was a minister of the gospel of Jesus Christ. He was talking to his friends in the shop about God and they were all talking about a lot of different things as he was cutting a man's hair. I remember them laughing and having such a good time and were really enjoying themselves but I was so sad and hurt.

Dixon stopped cutting the man's hair and said, "Son, is something wrong?" I looked up at him and said, "Yes, there is something wrong but I'd rather not talk about it." He said okay and he was going to finish this customer's haircut and whoever else needed one. Then he asked if I wanted one so I said "Yes, sir, I would."

"Since you will be the last one to get a haircut tonight," he said, "I will go ahead and close the shop. If you want to talk about anything, you are welcome to do so." He was such a nice man. I could feel a presence about him, that he spent a lot of time in the presence of God.

You see, in the part of the country where I was raised, in the south, I was taught we were not to be around black people, not to do anything with them or be friends with them. They were a different race of people and we were not to be involved with "that kind of people." I was taught that way all my life so I had never been around them or talked to them much at all. I was not taught that a black man could be so nice to a white person, instead I was taught they would not want to be nice to any white people. I didn't know how to accept his kindness and didn't know if it was a trick or something.

Friend, God was going to use this man to literally rip the prejudice out of me and show me that God can be in any race, in any heart.

Everyone had his haircut and left. It was just Dixon and me in the shop now. I got in the barber chair and he started cutting my hair. I thought he was going to start asking a lot of questions again about what was wrong with me and I was going to feel uncomfortable. He didn't do that at all. The most amazing thing happened. As he was cutting my hair he sang an old gospel song about his Lord. As he sang I remembered the words in the song. As he sang, I remembered the words in the song, "Every Day With Jesus Is Sweeter Than the Day Before."

It was only a few years since I had been saved. Oh, I knew what he was singing about and the tears came to my eyes. He didn't have to ask me to talk anymore, I wanted to talk to him. I felt he knew God as I knew God so I began telling him about coming home finding the trailer gone, mom was gone and dad was gone. I told him about my alcoholic father and what I had been going through. I told him how hard my mother's life was and that I quit school to go to work so I could help her.

The first thing he wanted to do, yes this black man, one of these black people that I was taught was so mean and wicked, these black people who don't like white people, said, "Son, I know what we should do."

I looked up at him and asked, "What?"

"Let's take it to our heavenly Father," he said. That statement grabbed me. I couldn't believe he was so concerned that he wasn't just going to pat me on the shoulder and say it was going to be all right, he was going to do something about it.

We prayed and when we finished, he said, "I have a suggestion but you can do what you want." I love the way he said it. He said, "I have this barbershop with a little room in the back. Sometimes I come here and stay all night. I have a bed and a table in there, a place that is nice and warm. My wife and I have a house on the other side of town and this room is empty, so if you don't want to go to those people next door in the trailer park and don't have any place to go, then why don't you just stay here tonight? I don't mind, I don't mind at all. I love talking with you so I'll tell you something I will try to do if you decide to stay here."

"But I don't have any money," I told him. "Not enough to pay you right now. I'm working at Burger King but I don't have enough to pay you." Dixon said "You don't have to pay me anything."

It kept running through my mind, a black man, and a black man doesn't want to give him anything. Isn't it awful that we have this kind of misconception in our mind of a race of people? It is so ridiculous now that I look back and think about it. Most people become prejudiced because they are hurt, and they have held unforgiveness in their heart. The Bible says there's no way you can prosper with unforgiveness in your heart, because if you can't forgive your brother you can't be forgiven yourself. I don't want to ever live with that kind of prejudice again. Praise the Lord!

This kind man let me stay in his room in the back of his barbershop. I was surprised he let me stay there all night and trusted me when he did not know me. The next morning when he came to open up the shop, he said, "Well, I'm not going to stay open very long today, son, there is something I would like to do for you. I'm going to take you out and we're going to have a real good meal. You name the place where you want to go." Then he said, "I want to buy you a suit of clothes. Is that okay? Get you some pants, a shirt and some shoes." I could not believe it. Then he said, "There is one more thing I would like to do for you if you will let me." "What is that sir?" I asked. "I would like to try to find your mother and your father and help you," he said.

Tears came to my eyes. I thought to myself, this man is for real. What would make him be this way to a white person? It was the love of God that was in his heart. The man told me he was going to close up shop in the middle of the day and we were going to take off and see what we could do. It would take a long time to tell you everything he did; but let me put it this way, for two solid weeks every day this man searched and looked, spent his money, his gas and time talking to everyone he could trying to find my mother and father.

We found my mother first. Lillie had moved into a small, old apartment in Brownsville, Kentucky. The apartments were in bad shape but they were very cheap and it was all she could afford. It was close to where her people lived and she was able to find a job. Mother opened the door when Dixon knocked and I never will forget how glad I was to see her. I was wondering what happened, what story she would tell me.

When she saw Dixon, she didn't know what to think. I could tell by the expression on her face she was so scared she was about to shut the door. She had been raised with this mentality of prejudice and didn't know any better. She was so upset seeing me with a black man who asked if we could come in. She did let us in the door a little then Mom put her arms around me, we hugged and began talking.

She explained to me she thought I was with my dad and that she was going to come and get me when she got things straightened out and could afford to. Then she looked at Dixon and I told her I had been staying in his barbershop and that he had been so kind to me. She could not grasp that I was talking in good terms about this black man.

Suddenly she looked at me and said, "If you would like to stay with him, it's okay." She was sure I was going to say "no." Then I said, "Okay." Dixon looked at me then looked at her and he knew I gave the right answer at that time.

Dixon and I went down the stairway and out the door. I remember my heart was beating fast because I was walking away from the woman who had raised me, the only one I had ever known and cherished in my heart more than anyone else in the world. I knew I was standing up for what was right.

We walked out the door and got in the car. As we drove away and started down the road, Dixon told me he had information about where my father was and we would go see about him.

We arrived at my father's place. He lived in a little trailer on a plantation out in the country in a wooded area. The little one room trailer was in Kentucky's Edmonson County. All it had was a refrigerator and stove that were falling apart and a tiny bed just big enough for one person. Part of the floor had rotted out. Yes, it was that bad.

Dixon knocked on the door and when dad opened it, we noticed he was drunk. There were liquor bottles lying all over the place. Being drunk, my dad didn't mind that Dixon was black. This terrible drunk who was misunderstood by all who did not know him did not think bad of Dixon because he was black.

He put his arms around me and was so glad to see me. My dad then staggered back to his bed and sat down leaning against the wall. He told me he thought I was with my mother. Dixon looked around the room seeing the filth, the whiskey bottles and the refrigerator that was falling apart. Wilbur went to the refrigerator and there was no food except cabbage. He had boiled cabbage and ate on it for over a week. He wanted to spend grocery money to buy his liquor.

Dixon knew this was not a place where I should be left but he didn't know how to say it. He knew that I loved my father and he tried to find a way to get me to leave.

He turned to me and said, "You know what? We have to go downtown and do some things but we can come back if you like." So I told my dad I would be back later. We went outside and Dixon told me, "I can't leave you here. You are a good boy and you are going to be a great man, do great things for God. This I know, I cannot leave you here." "Are you sure I shouldn't stay here?" I asked. "He is the only Father I have." He looked at me and said, "No, he's not. No, he's not." "Okay," I said. "I trust you."

I told dad goodbye and I would be back to see him. Because of the condition he was in, he did not understand a lot. We left and I will never forget that day, the day I walked away from both of the people who had loved and raised me, who had taught me everything I had ever known. However, since I met God, I wanted to do what was right and wanted to find a better life than what we had. I knew if I didn't reach out for it in some way, it was never going to come. I knew God was now bringing me to a place where I would have to learn how to trust and believe in Him to guide my life.

God changed my life that day and brought me to a place of faith I had not been since I was first saved. Showing me that now I was going to have to learn how to live by faith, not depending on people. I had so much to learn.

Dixon brought me back to the barbershop and I stayed in that back room. Oh, what I was about to learn. This wonderful man I have been telling you about made some of the most dramatic changes in my life that have ever been made just simply by watching him and the wonderful things he did for God.

Dixon was a great minister of God who went to every church where God opened a door for him and preached with all his heart about Jesus Christ. He wanted everybody he came into contact with to be saved. If they were sick, he wanted them healed, if they were worried or depressed, he wanted them to be full of joy. He would take whatever the devil handed people and would try to destroy it so God would get glory from it. I never met anyone with such unction and hunger to do God's work.

I was young then and not ready for all that. I didn't want to bring my life to the place where I truly wanted to be with God like Dixon was. I thought he was overdoing it and now wish I had looked at him much differently then.

This man of faith, this man of God I was around preached the gospel and taught me many things. He went into a home where they kept people who were put out with no place to go and then bring teenagers home with him. He told them about God, looked to find them a job so they could get out on their own and start their lives. He also brought people in off the street and make meals for them. He also bought lots of food; more than he needed for himself, then pray asking God send him people who needed to eat and they would just show up. It was amazing.

Dixon walked by faith. He wanted to help me find a job so I could get out on my own. Not only that, this man brought me to his home, wanting me to stay there instead of the barbershop. His wife was not very pleased with that and was so upset with him that she told him if he chose to do something like this, she would not stay with him anymore.

They finally ended up in divorce with him moving to Columbus, Indiana and I went with him. He was going to start a new life working for Cummins Engine. He had a good job and was still doing his ministry and helping people. I decided at that point to go into the military. I thought maybe I could get an education and be better off when I came out. I thought going into the service I would not be a burden to anyone so I decided to sign up for the Army National Guard but there was some time before I had to report for duty. I felt better about things now as I would not be a burden or cause any problems in case Dixon would go back to his wife.

He was satisfied he had done what was right and what God

wanted him to do. He did everything he could to reconcile with his wife but she chose not to but God was with him.

> *If ye fulfill the royal law according to the scripture, thou shalt love thy neighbour as thyself, ye do well. (9) But if ye have respect to persons, ye commit sin, and are convinced of the law as transgressors.*
> James 2:8-9

Chapter 8

DEVASTATED LOVE

*Behold, thou art fair, my love, Behold,
thou art fair; thou hast doves' eyes.*
Song of Solomon 1:15

WHEN WE WERE in Columbus, Indiana, I had to leave for the service. I met a young lady named Connie who was the most wonderful person I had ever met in my life and we spent a lot of time together. She was the first girlfriend I was really close to, close enough that I was trying to decide if I wanted to be with her forever. I walked two miles to her home and two miles back quite often.

We had finally made the decision to get married when I got out of the service. Her father and Dixon worked at Cummins Engine so it was almost guaranteed that I could get a job there when I came out of the service. We planned to start our lives together and then for once, we could have a normal life. I thought of that the whole time while in the service.

We were writing each other continuously. It was a wonderful relationship writing back and forth knowing that as soon as I got out, this wonderful thing was going to happen.

One night while in the service, we were driving our convoy of trucks out on the edge of a cliff and I could not see to drive so we had to stop. I told my sergeant I could not see, that I have trouble with this one eye. Of course, he did not believe me and thought I should just keep driving. Finally they realized I was having trouble seeing so they had me get my eyes checked. They found I was clinically blind in that one eye. When they had admitted me into the service they said there was nothing wrong with that eye, but now my eye was so bad, if I wanted out of the service I could leave with an honorable discharge, which I took, because I wanted to get home and get married.

I spent four years in the service and they let me out with an honorable discharge. Now I was probably the happiest man on the planet. I was packing my bags, anxious to get home to Connie, to prepare for our marriage and to have the life I had always wanted.

I will never forget flying home and driving to her house, she didn't know I was coming. When I stepped out of the car and she came out of the house, she ran to me and we held each other until we almost fell to the ground. It was wonderful. It was the first time in my life I felt loved by a woman that way. She told me about how everything was ready for us to get married. I went to Dixon and told him I was out of the service and stayed with him. He was happy for me.

One day when I was downtown I saw a friend I had not seen for a while. He came up to me and said, "Did you know Connie has been seeing another man while you were away in the service?" I could not believe him. "This can't be so," I said. I knew I must confront her to see if it was true. I just could not see Connie doing this and if she tells me it is not true, I will believe her. When I asked her about it she had a strange look and said "I wouldn't do something like that."

The next week I was downtown and another friend came to me and said, "Oh, I thought Connie was seeing someone else." I knew this person very well and that he wouldn't lie to me. So I went back and confronted Connie again. This time she broke down crying and said, "Yes, I have been seeing someone else but I was wrong."

Of course, I believe now that I should have forgiven her. If I stayed with her or not, I should have forgiven her, but in my heart, I was so angry and hurt. I had so many emotions I didn't know which to accept. I told her the marriage was off and we gave back the rings we had exchanged. She cried and I went back home to Dixon. Her parents brought her to where Dixon and I were and tried to talk to me but I refused and shut the door. She was crying and saying she was sorry but for some reason I kept saying "no." I felt that if she would do this now, she could do it again.

Friend, I cannot know if she would or not. We really shouldn't judge people that way. We have a right to make a decision to do what we want but we really should not pass judgment on others. Now I see that and realize I lived with unforgiveness in my heart for several years over that and struggled with it. I would not have had to live with that if I had released it, now I understand.

If I could do it over again, I would have forgiven her whether I stayed with her or not. At that time though, I could not do it and we went our separate ways.

I went into a state of depression I had never been in before. I had experienced not being loved by my parents and not being accepted in the family in certain ways. I had experienced some hard times being alone and being taken in by a black family. I had experienced a lot of things but I had never experienced the hurt that comes from a relationship when you think you are going to bind yourself together, to be married. I had never experienced what it is like to lose that. Then I realized it must be like what Dixon experienced when he lost his wife.

Dixon knew this was happening to me and that he had to do something. He had a week long revival in Burkesville, Kentucky, where his sister lived and he kept begging me to go with him. He wanted me to help him by playing the guitar. It would be in a different part of the country and something I would enjoy. He talked me into it finally so we went to Burkesville to his revival.

> *For if ye forgive men their trespasses, your heavenly Father will also forgive you.*
> Matthew 6:14

Chapter 9

THE GETAWAY

Preach the word, be instant in season, out of season, reprove, rebuke, exhort, with all longsuffering and doctrine.
2 Timothy 4:2

Now I am at Burkesville, Kentucky, and the revival is planned. I am still depressed but it helped to be in a different place around some different people. I met Dixon's sister and oh, what a wonderful woman she was. And guess what? Her husband was an alcoholic. Can you believe it? She was the most wonderful lady that loved the Lord. She was like Dixon and just glowed with God. She could not wait until the revival.

She was not prejudiced and when she met me she loved me so much and made me so welcome in her home. "Oh, we're going to have one of the best revivals we have ever had," she said. "I couldn't wait until my brother got here." We had the revival and it went great and many were saved and so many wonderful things happened. Then I met a lady in Burkesville named Elizabeth. She lived with her grandmother and grandfather and had been raised by them most of the time.

Her brother was playing basketball and invited some of us to play. He told me about his sister and suggested I come over so I had dinner with them and then met Elizabeth. Something wonderful had now happened. It was amazing to me how I could have gone from that period of depression then instantly turned around feeling like something good was going to happen in my life. Connie was now totally out of my life and I was convinced she is not who God wanted me to be with. Now is the time to date this new lady.

Elizabeth was raised in the country, a wonderful cook and very beautiful. She had much kindness in her heart, a lady who seemed to understand a lot of the things we talked about. It finally came to the point where I had to decide if I would stay near Burkesville where I could see Elizabeth or go back to where Dixon was.

I found a job in a sewing factory in that town and decided to take that job and stay in Burkesville. After I decided to stay in Burkesville, we just kept getting closer and closer, something wonderful began to happen.

He hath made everything beautiful in His time.
Ecclesiastes 3:11

Chapter 10

MATRIMONY IN THE MAKING

*Whoso findeth a wife findeth a good thing,
and obtaineth favour of the Lord.*
Proverbs 18:22

I AM SURE YOU have guessed it by now by the title itself, Elizabeth and I decided to get married. We did get married and several years later had our first child, a little girl we named Tausha. This little girl was the most wonderful, most beautiful and most glorious thing I had ever experienced in my life. She was everything I lived for other than Jesus Christ. She was the dearest thing to my heart. There are no words I could use to explain what this little girl did to my life when she was born. I loved her so much, loved coming home watching her come to me and I loved taking her places. Sometimes she would get mad and have her little fits but it didn't matter, she brought so much happiness to my life.

A few years later we had a little boy we named Jeremy. Now the second most precious thing in my life had come. I'm not trying to say that I made a difference in my children or that I loved one more than the other. I am just saying that he came along after Tausha and now another wonderful thing came into my life the same way and I loved him just as much. These children gave me a joy in my life I had never experienced.

Now that I had my wife and two children, it seemed as though it just couldn't be any better. My job didn't pay well and we struggled financially, but you know friend, I found out in that relationship that money isn't everything. I know we need money and it's a great blessing to have it, but there are other things more valuable than money. Like having a good family life, a good wife and good children. Oh, that's a blessing money could never buy.

We moved into our first house out in the country and were renting because the job I had didn't pay well. Next door to us was an elderly couple who worked in the fields for a man who owned the plantation. He also owned the house we lived in and the house they lived in but I didn't work on the plantation. I watched these people as they worked in the fields and thought to myself, how could these people work that way? I don't know how old they were but guessed them to be in their late seventies. They raised a tobacco crop and a humongous garden. They didn't do it with much equipment, just hard labor. I wanted to get to know these people.

The first thing I learned about them after we moved in was they liked music. Their porch had a small radio and I will never forget the song playing, it was "I'm Working on a Building." Some of the lines were: "I'm working on a building, I'm working on a building, I'm working on a building for my Lord, for my Lord. It's a Holy Ghost building, it's a Holy Ghost building, it's a Holy Ghost building for my Lord, for my Lord." They would come out on the porch and listen to that song over and over. I heard that song so many times I was wondering if they had any other music.

I decided to go next door and introduce myself since we were now neighbors. I told them I heard their song playing again and again. They said, "Yes, don't you just love that song?" "Yes," I said. "It's a good song."

"Oh, we are, we are working on a building and it's for our Lord," they said. "It is really a Holy Ghost building. We have the Holy Ghost within us."

Now I was around someone who talked about other things that I had not experienced in God. They talked about speaking in tongues and about dancing in the Spirit. These people were not educated and I thought they probably don't know much of what they are talking about. I know there is a Holy Ghost and the Holy Ghost drew me when I was saved, but these people talked about it differently. They said it caused them to speak in tongues; in another language and made them literally dance all over the porch.

A lot of people ran them down, some even said they were not in their right minds. And I thought to myself, you know, am I going to look at these people the way they talk about them in town or am I going to try to get to know them?

One day at home God dealt with my heart, He spoke to me and said, "I want you to go spend some time with these people. Just talk with them." I tell you I had the most glorious experience.

One man had a hump in his back from working so hard bent over harvesting his tobacco crop. I thought to myself, it's a shame a man of his age having to work this way. How could this man who owned this plantation live with his conscience? I know he didn't give them much money because they didn't even have much to eat. They got most of the things they ate from their garden and I thought how could this be that someone would treat them this way.

But I had the most wonderful experience by living in that

place. I believe God had me there to learn about some of the gifts of the Spirit, especially tongues. I had not been taught about it and these people did not have enough knowledge to teach it, but they lived it. You could hear them in the fields working and then suddenly begin to speak in tongues. The elderly woman would shout a little bit and dance a little bit raising her hands to God. This happened quite often.

Suddenly God revealed something to me. He said, "You remember when you asked the question? How could these elderly people work like this, how could they stand doing this kind of work? It's because my Holy Spirit takes care of them." That just turned me inside out. Now for the first time I saw they had something I never experienced. The people who said this nice elderly couple had something wrong with them were wrong. It was quite the opposite, they had something *right* with them, it was the Holy Ghost, a real experience of the Holy Ghost and His power.

I decided to spend more time talking with them and ask where they learned these things. They told me how they learned this in church. They went to a Pentecostal Church of course, and this was the way they had been taught all their lives, even as children. Their experience of God was so real, it sustained them at a time when most others would not have survived.

God taught me great lessons by living next door to these people. One of the lessons He taught me was to never look on the outside for God in a person because God is on the inside. A person may seem to be very knowledgeable but that does not make them greater than God. He looks on the heart and that is where He reigns. He is looking for those who will humble themselves as little children and be dependent on Him. These are the ones God gives power to.

While I lived there I learned a great lesson in that. There was a wonderful thing that happened to me I would like to share with you. These neighbors decided to have some services at their house and were going to come up with a way to make it happen. They didn't have a lot of friends because most people considered them not smart or intelligent, that something was wrong with them. They wanted to invite people who went to their church and there were not many people who attended their church. These people had been praying for their son who was at least in his forties, a man who did not believe in God as they did. He looked at them as if something was wrong with them but he did love his mother and father. They prayed earnestly for their son to be saved and the father prayed that he did not want to die until he saw God save his son. These people who you may have looked at as not important, old people seemingly not good for anything but being used in the field, to finish their work on the farm and die, but God was doing something great with them.

For example, one day their son came to the house when they were having the service both inside and outside the house. When people heard about the service from others, they came too, it was unbelievable. They were expecting five or six people to come and they had about thirty, which was a lot of people to them. It was also unbelievable because in the past, people had rejected them. But the people came and they had a service during which there was a message. I was in my house and could hear the people as there was so much commotion going on so I decided to go over there.

People were shouting, lying on the floor, praying and speaking in tongues. It was the presence of God all over the house. That old house had cracks in the walls, the wind was blowing through and the furniture was falling apart but God was in that house. The message that night reached the man's son who fell on his knees, repented giving his life to the Lord.

I thought to myself, God heard that man's prayers in spite of what anyone thought of him. But the most wonderful thing that happened was how it affected my life changing me. In about two months their son came into their house weeping and said, "The Lord has called me to preach the Gospel!" I thought his father would never stop praising the Lord, I said he's going to get hoarse. It didn't matter, he knew it was God. These people who seemed so insignificant to the world had now helped turn a man who didn't care about God into one who would preach the Gospel and reach hundreds, if not thousands of souls in the future.

Oh, how we overlook the significance of someone with Jesus. That man became a great minister and sometimes came over to his parents' house. Even though they only had six or seven people, he preached out on the porch because he wanted so badly to obey God. Eventually it began to grow and he was able to go elsewhere and preach the Gospel. He has reached hundreds of souls now, even way back in the country where you thought it couldn't be done, but he did because of his heart and his love for God.

All I can say is this, the experience I had with those people who everybody thought was out of their minds, was one of the greatest experiences I ever had. I learned the lesson to not look on the outside for the power of God.

But the Lord said unto Samuel, Look not on his countenance, or on the height of his stature, because I have refused him: for the Lord seeth not as man seeth, for man looketh on the outward appearance, but the Lord looketh on the heart.
1 Samuel 16:7

Chapter 11

THE UNSELFISH HERO

Blessed is he that considereth the poor, the Lord will deliver him in time of trouble.
Psalms 41:1

YOU KNOW, I couldn't wait to tell you this story. There was a member of our neighbor's family called "Bootie" who was deaf nor could he speak. He decided to come live with them because they were having such a hard time taking care of the tobacco field and raising their food. They were actually injuring themselves, even though God was taking care of them, but it was just a matter of time. God knew they needed help. Bootie was also not in good physical condition and had been staying with other members of his family.

They called him Bootie because he wore these big rubber boots that came all the way up to his knees, the kind that fishermen wear when they wade out in the water. I always wondered why in the world he wanted to wear those boots.

After I watched him a while, I found out why. He worked in the muddy tobacco fields, even in the rain. He knew those boots would protect his feet and he was in the field more than he was in the house or anywhere else. That was his way of life, all he knew or had ever experienced. He would not part with his rubber boots and that is how he got the name Bootie.

It does not do justice to call this man a hero. Even though most people had written him off in their lives, he was a hero to me. Bootie would come over to our house early in the morning most of the time. He loved to hunt and go back in the woods to hunt squirrel and rabbit. He liked to do any kind of hunting but he didn't have a gun and could not afford to buy a gun. He would come over to our house early in the morning on weekends when he knew I was off from work and point his hands like a gun. I knew he wanted me to take my gun out and go back in the woods with him. He simply loved that.

I went to the woods with him and he could not hear the gun when it fired but it amazed him to see the gun fire. If you shot a squirrel and it fell to the ground, he was so amazed over it. He was an expert at finding them because he had spent his life in the wilderness. I would go rabbit and squirrel hunting and it made him so happy to think he had somebody who would go out and enjoy activities with him.

Bootie could never talk to me, never heard a word I said, and didn't know sign language. However, we could communicate as well as with anyone who could speak. I knew what he meant by his gestures, the expressions on his face when he did or did not like something, when he wanted to do something and when he did not. I actually loved Bootie as if he was my brother and was getting close to this little short man who wasn't big or strong. He was what most people would call a weakling but he worked long hours. He would continue to work long hours when others would have stopped. He could work from morning until almost dark, sometimes not stopping to eat. I thought it was amazing that he had so much stamina.

There is something I would like to tell you about this hero of mine. Every weekend after we got back from hunting, he would almost always, every weekend, run over to his house and find something even if it was a small piece of candy, an orange or a muffin, or whatever he had to eat that was sweet, and bring it over to my children. He could hardly wait to give that to my kids. They loved to see Bootie because he always brought them something. If he did not bring them something to eat, he had some little something he had made from a piece of wood. He had something for those children every weekend that we lived as neighbors. They would take what Bootie offered and be so happy.

My small son would reach out to thank Bootie and all he could hug was the top of Bootie's rubber boots. Friend, that man who could not hear or speak had something more powerful than hearing or speech. He had a heart that could speak and a heart that could hear. When I saw that, I thought of a lot of things about God.

We can communicate with God without saying a word. We can show God that we love Him and we can pay attention and be willing to listen to God. When I watched Bootie and all of his wonderful characteristics and thought about how he had been put out by so many people who didn't realize what a wonderful person he was, I realized something. God loved him as much as he loved me and I should love Bootie as much as I loved anyone else on this earth. I made up my mind I was going to do just that so I took him fishing. We would go for rides in the car back into the country and to other parts of the woods he had never seen before. He was so happy because someone had just spent some time with him.

Winter came and snow was on the ground. We had one of the largest snows I had ever seen since I was a child in Kentucky. No one was actually prepared when the snow came. Where we lived, we had a wood stove and we were almost out of wood. I was laid off my job at the sewing factory. It really looked bad. My two children were getting hungry, I was trying to find work and my car was falling apart. I was going out searching for work and there was so much snow I could not travel anywhere, couldn't do anything. I prayed and asked God to show me what to do. I knew He was going to do something but I never dreamed He would do it the way He did. I thought if only he would send me a truck that could travel in that snow. I kept believing and thinking that God was going to provide a job some way.

One morning when I woke up, Bootie came over and knocked on the door. We went out behind the property where they raised tobacco and he pointed to the top of the trees. I looked up and wondered what he was trying to show me. He took his hand up the tree and back down and then he would put his arms around the tree trying to tell me it was a huge tree. Then he swung his hand like he was going to chop it. He was telling me that I could have that tree. Of course I didn't have a saw or an ax and neither did Bootie. What good did it do for us to be trapped and not be able to have that tree for firewood? I went back home.

The next morning I woke up to a strange sound. It was really loud and getting louder and then not so loud and then loud again. I realized it sounded like a chainsaw. I hurried out of bed, dressed and went outside. There was Bootie with a chainsaw. The saw looked bigger than he did and I really felt sorry for him. I went out and took the saw from him and I saw that he was freezing. "Bootie, you have to go into the house," I said. I was pointing to the house and he didn't want to leave. I finally pried him from the chainsaw and got him inside to keep him from freezing. He had cut enough wood to keep us warm for a couple of nights. I just could not believe it.

He went home that evening and we went to bed that night. The next morning the sun was shining when we woke up. It was shining on the front porch. I walked into the living room and looked through the window. Everywhere I looked there was wood! It covered every bit of our porch. Bootie had gone back out at night while we were sleeping. He had been cutting and chopping and working until he had completely filled our porch with wood. We are talking about zero weather. This was enough wood to last us most of the winter, if not all winter. I had to thank him so much. I knew it was Bootie. No one else could have done it.

When I went next door to thank him, the elderly couple answered the door and said Bootie wanted to talk to me. I went in the room where he was lying in bed. When I heard him wheezing, I had no doubt that he had pneumonia. I knew that he was very sick. I leaned down close to him and told him I was there. He was so weak he could hardly hold my hand.

I rushed to my house and made a poultice out of Vicks salve and put different things on him that I thought might help him, hoping it would loosen some of the phlegm in his chest. I could see that it was not doing any good. I thought, "Oh, my God! I can't get Bootie to the hospital because of the snow." What are we going to do? I got my car out and started it and decided I was going to have to try or Bootie was going to die.

To this day, I do not know how I got out of there unless it was just the Angels who helped me make it through that snow. I drove to the main highway and took Bootie to the hospital.

The next day Bootie died. The person the world thought so little of was a hero to me. I believe one day when I walk into the kingdom of heaven I will see Bootie. I don't know what he will have on his feet but I know he won't be wearing those old rubber boots. I know he will be able to speak to me and hear me. In my eyes he is still a hero.

I learned a lesson from that man. What was the lesson? Never write a person off because of a weakness they have in their life. He might have been what most people may have called a weakling and he couldn't talk or hear. He worked hard in the fields. He wasn't a man with great finances or with a great education. He seemed weak as far as the world was concerned, but think about this for a moment. He saved the life of the elderly couple next door by doing the work they couldn't do. It was probably harder on him than it was on them. He took his weakness and made a difference. He made sure that my two children were kept warm when I had not known what to do and was about to give up. This man who seemed weak did not give up. He used what strength he had to make sure that we were warm that winter. I don't call this man weak, I call this man a hero.

I believe there are a lot of heroes God has out there that we overlook. We sometimes think they are not even needed in our life. If God showed me anything in this, He showed me that we need each other regardless of our weaknesses.

Greater love hath no man than this, that a man lay down his life for his friends.
John 15:13

Chapter 12

THE STRANGER
WHO WAS SORRY

*The Spirit of the Lord is upon me, because he
hath anointed me to preach the gospel to the poor;
he hath sent me to heal the brokenhearted.*
Luke 4:18

SUMMERTIME HAD COME and the flowers were blooming. I was back to work and everything seemed wonderful. I was enjoying my life with my family. We had a stranger come to our house to visit. One evening when I was home from work, a knock came at the door. I opened the door and there stood a very attractive elderly lady. I would guess her to be in her late seventies or early eighties. She had a very sad look on her face.

When I asked her what she wanted, she asked me if my name was Glen Connors and I said, "Yes, that's my name." "I would like to talk to you," she said. "There is something very important I would like to talk to you about. I need to come in and talk with you if that is ok." "Sure," I said. "Come in and sit down. I would be glad to hear what it is you have to say."

The woman sat at my kitchen table. My wife was cooking

something to eat and I saw that the lady was sad and I wondered why she wanted to talk to me. Suddenly she broke into tears. I felt so sorry for her but I didn't know what to do. I did not know the woman and I didn't know what to say.

After she stopped crying, she said, "I guess I shouldn't beat around the bush but just come out and say it." "What is it you are trying to say?" I asked her. "I am your grandmother," she said.

I didn't know what to think. I have never been so shocked in all my life. I had never seen my real grandmother. This was my father's mother.

"I have to apologize and tell you some things that are very sad right now," she said. "My husband's name was Homer and he just died. We lived about twelve miles from your house. Every weekend I would see you down town in Brownsville, Kentucky. I knew you were my grandson but I could not say anything to you. Lots of times when you passed by, I wondered how you were doing and how your life was going. I knew my daughter-in-law gave you away, you were in a home where you were very happy and didn't want to bother you when you were a child. I did not want to interfere with the family you were in but now that you are grown and have children, I thought about coming to see you. I just didn't know if that would cause a problem in your life now."

I couldn't believe what I was hearing. I couldn't take my eyes off this woman. I don't know how to tell you how wonderful it was to be looking at my grandmother. One part of me was so happy I wanted to hug her; the other part was upset because she had kept herself from me. Why did she keep herself from me?

She said that her husband, my grandfather Homer, had gotten an infection in his leg and it turned into gangrene. They could do no more for him and his body became infected and he died. She told me she knew when this happened she had to come and talk to me.

"I want to make you welcome in my home," she said. "I want you to come see me. I want to apologize for all those years that I did not talk to you, did not communicate with you. I know now that I should have regardless of any problems it might have brought you. Now that my husband has died, I see that I need everyone in our family. Would you please forgive me? Will you come see me?"

She gave me a hug and I returned her hug and she walked out the door. After she left I walked the floor for about two hours. My mind was going in circles. "I can't believe this!" I said. "That was my grandmother!"

Where Lillie raised me could not have been more than twenty-five or thirty miles from where they lived. All the times she saw me as a child and never once tried to tell me she was my grandmother. I was so puzzled. I tried to decide if I should go see her or not. The devil was telling me not to go but The Lord was telling me to go see her. Would it hurt me more? I was so mixed up. I wanted to know her so badly. I decided I could find out more about my family, things I wanted to know, through my grandmother. I should get to know my grandmother.

I asked the Lord to forgive me for not going quicker than I did. The Lord kept impressing upon me to visit her but I fought it and did not go because of the resentment in my heart. I finally gave up and said okay, I'll visit her this weekend. She had left me her telephone number, so I called to tell her I was coming.

Someone else answered the phone and when I asked to speak to my grandmother, she said, "Your grandmother is dead."

I just shook my head. All I could think about was God tried to tell me to go. Friend, have you ever had that to happen? When you disobeyed the presence of the Lord in your heart and known the misery that comes when you see the results of your disobedience? Sometimes I wonder if there was a purpose for me not to see her again.

Although I was not able to see her and find out anything concerning our family, I do know this. I am so glad she had the nerve to come to see me and make things right with me. I know I did not get to spend any time with my grandmother or my grandfather on my father's side, but a great lesson came from this experience. I believe it was this, If we have anything we need to get right with someone, we should not wait until the last moment. We don't have to live live in fear of it or what might happen if we try to make it right.

I learned from my grandmother coming to me. That experience taught me not to wait if I have something against someone. We never know when it may be the last opportunity to fix things. Sometimes it doesn't appear clear enough to us that there will be heartache for us to carry around if we continue to hold things in that we should let go of. I learned a great lesson from Grandmother. If I have anything in my heart that I need to settle with anyone, I should do it quickly and get it over with, get it out and let it be gone. Don't be afraid to do it, that is the way God intends for us to be.

> *Therefore to him that knoweth to do good
> and doeth it not, to him it is sin.*
> James 4:17

Chapter 13

THE TORNADO AND THE TWIG

*He that dwelleth in the secret place of the most
High shall abide under the shadow of the Almighty.*
Psalms 91:1

I WAS OFFERED a new job in Bowling Green, Kentucky with a company called Holly Carburetor. I was so excited and happy about it because it had better benefits and paid quite a bit more on the hour. After I worked at this job for a while, Elizabeth and I decided to get a loan, buy some property and get a mobile home. Over in Edmonson County we found two acres of the most beautiful land we had ever seen. It was wooded, full of tall pine trees and very beautiful. At the very end of the property was a bluff and a very deep valley. There was a blue mist in the bottom of the valley created by certain trees that grew there. It was the most beautiful property we had ever seen.

We bought our new home and put it on the land and we were enjoying our happy life to the fullest. I was coming to a place where God was dealing with me to spend more time with Him and to get involved in the church more. I started going to Cove Hollow Baptist Church there in Edmonson County and I was trying to learn everything I could about God. Behind our property were miles and miles of beautiful woods. When I went down into the valley, I took a cane with me and hooked it on a tree to pull myself back up. I could not go down into or up out of the valley without the cane. I went into that valley every chance I got because it was so beautiful with waterfalls, flowers and so much beauty. The farther I walked the more beauty I could see. There was one precious place that I especially loved right on the very end of my property and as you stood on top of the bluff, you could see for miles. There was a large area of green moss at the edge of the bluff that was like a carpet and when you walked on it you would sink down, it was so wonderful. In the middle of that moss was a very small tree, not even as tall as me. The pretty little tree had tiny branches and that is where I chose to go and pray. The moss was so soft on my knees and I could just kneel or lie there and pray.

At that time I had a little black and white mixed Border Collie named Shep. He was a wonderful pet and often went back in the woods with me. When I knelt to pray in that moss Shep would come up beside me. He went wherever I went and was so much company. I enjoyed going back there to pray and spend time with God. Sometimes I would take my Bible and study there. I was having a relationship with God and His Word in prayer. I was learning so many things from those times and from the messages I was hearing at church. It was a time when I was growing in the word of God.

One day when I arrived home after praying in that special spot, I had a cane with me I chopped from the root of a tree and it was a rather unique cane. I liked it and usually took it with me when I went out in the woods. When I finished praying that day, I decided to go home but something spoke to me and I knew it was God. He was telling me to take that cane and hang it on the little tree in the mossy area, which I thought was strange and I wondered why the Lord would tell me to hang that cane on the limb of that little tree. It doesn't make any sense, no reason at all unless God has a purpose for me to leave it there that I don't understand yet, but I knew He wanted me to. The branches on that little tree were so small, when I tried to hang the cane on one of the limbs, it would bounce and could barely support it. But I still hung it on the limb like the voice within me said. Shep and I started on our way back home where I had underpinned our mobile home and fixed it the way we wanted. We were very pleased, everything was good; our home, our land and my job was going well.

That evening I looked up at the sky and it was cloudy, as if it was going to rain, but I didn't think it looked very bad. I sat on the couch looking out my window then laid my head down thinking I would go to sleep. In less than three seconds one of the most severe storms I have ever experienced in my life hit. The wind started blowing against the sides of our home shaking it from the foundation and I shook too, like never before. I thought to myself, my God, where is this coming from? Right over the top of our home was a tornado which was really high in the air but the wind from it was tearing everything to pieces.

I looked out the kitchen window and trees that you could put your arms around twice and never get all the way around them were bending over touching the ground, trees. It was twisting them apart like someone taking a small pencil twisting it and breaking it.

As I watched, I knew I should grab my kids and get out of there or we would be killed. I grabbed Tausha, Elizabeth grabbed Jeremy and we tried to open the door but it would not. I tried with all the strength I had but could not open it. So I laid down on my back trying to push with my feet while Elizabeth pushed from the top. Finally, when we got the door open, I have never seen such forceful wind. We knew our lives were in danger going out into that wind but also knew we would not make it if we stayed inside. We held on to the children and ran across the road to our neighbor's brick home. Trees were falling all around us, and thank God, they did not hit us.

We knocked on the neighbor's door and they screamed for us to come in. The door was unlocked and they were staying in the hallway. We made our way inside to the hallway and laid down. I decided to go to the door and see the storm which I know was a silly idea but I wanted to. I stood in front of the door and could not believe what was happening.

All of the pine trees around our mobile home were so big I'm not sure how to describe them. Pine trees get very tall and these trees began to bend from the force of the wind. All of the trees out front bent over our mobile home and stayed that way. The trees in the back bent the opposite way over our mobile home toward the front. It bent the trees both directions in such a way that our home was locked inside them and the wind could not blow it away. I didn't know this until the storm was gone, but if you bend a pine tree over and hold it that way long enough, it will stay that way.

Everything else on our two acres as well as the land behind ours as far as you could see was destroyed. I could not believe it. I watched the forceful wind doing that and thought, "We are going to die, that thing is going to turn and come this direction, and if it does, it's coming right through this house. This is our time. We are going to leave this world."

But that tornado did not come, instead it lifted and went down the road. Two houses down from us a man had come from visiting his father in Louisville, Kentucky and went in the house as the storm struck. He sat down on his couch and at that moment, a tree fell on his house killing him. Half of the homes on our road were destroyed by the tornado but my home was still being held on both sides by those trees. Every tree on those two acres had been destroyed but God protected our home. Later, we had news reporters and people from all over taking pictures. They could not believe the incredible sight of those trees protecting our home.

The mobile home was not harmed, not even a dent. Just some damage to the underpinning, but did not hurt the main structure at all. Amazing!

We stayed all night with our neighbors across the road. The next morning the storm had passed and it was a beautiful, clear, sunny day so we decided to go back home. We went back expecting to see it all torn to pieces inside, wondering what we were going to do. We had gone into debt for our home and we had insurance but still, it was the only home we had. We had to make a way through the trees to get inside. One of the trees had to be cut and pulled away so it wouldn't fall on it. When we got inside, we found not one item broken. The foundation and walls were okay too. I could hardly believe it.

Then there was something more amazing. I looked out the back window, the sun shining really bright and I saw parts of all those trees where they had been twisted off. It looked like somebody had just grabbed them and twisted them in two. There were twigs sticking up almost everywhere for two miles, little stubs with twists on the ends of them.

Then I saw something I could not believe. At the end of our property where the moss covered the ground, was that little tree, the only tree on my two acres that was not destroyed. "My God!" I thought. "How could that be?" That little twig of a tree, how in the world could it be standing when this force has torn up two acres of big trees? Then God reminded me, that is the place where I pray and I saw something even more incredible. It was a long way off, but it looked like that cane was still hanging and bouncing on the limb of that tree! It had not been blown off of that little limb! Trees that weighed literally tons were twisted and broken like pencils and this little cane is hanging on the limb of that tree in my place of prayer. Then I realized that place was not only important to me, God wanted to show me it was also important to Him. God respected that I had a prayer place and He was not going to let anything harm it. I believe He told me to put the cane on that limb and I believe He kept it on that limb. He knew the storm was coming and wanted to show me that He would protect what is His. This was another miracle I was privileged to see and I have never forgotten that day. You may not think it was a miracle but if you had seen the destruction that took place there and that cane still hanging on the little limb, you too would know it was a miracle.

We were able to sell all the wood on the property left by the storm and used the money to repair the land. While we lived there we had a wonderful life.

Here's the lesson I learned. God is our protector and when we make up our mind to put God in anything, to make Him a part of it using it for His glory, He is going to protect it.

Because thou has made the Lord, which is my refuge, even the most High, thy habitation. (10) There shall no evil befall thee neither shall any plague come nigh thy dwelling. (11) For He shall give His angels charge over thee, to keep thee in all thy ways.
Psalms 91:9-11

Chapter 14

FAME: THE DEVIL'S SPOTLIGHT

Pride goeth before destruction, and an haughty spirit before a fall. (19) Better it is to be of an humble spirit with the lowly, than to divide the spoil with the proud.
Proverbs 16:18-19

I DECIDED TO TRY to do something with my music. I was writing country songs at that time and I was also writing gospel songs. It seemed as though it was easier to get things done in the country music field than in the gospel field. I had written several country songs so I thought I would take a few of them to Nashville and see what could be done.

When I went to Nashville, all the doors I knocked on were shut. Nobody wanted to listen to me, I guess because I was unheard of. I spent quite a bit of money trying to get someone to listen to me but they did not want to listen. I was fairly discouraged about it and wondered why God wasn't helping me with this. I knew I had a talent and wondered why no one would recognize it.

I was still going to Cove Hollow Baptist Church when during a service there, a lady told my wife she was not the wife she should be and there were certain things she should not do. This hurt my wife so bad she decided not to go back to that church and I didn't know what to do. I knew my wife was right, not in quitting church, but that she had been done wrong. I didn't want to cause a commotion in the church so I talked to the pastor but it didn't do any good. No one tried to help or fix things with us. I felt this was wrong and I too was hurt. Instead of turning it over to God like I should, I thought I could take care of this problem. Have you ever done that? I failed because I was hurt and then discouraged, I felt if they didn't welcome my wife, I was not going there either. Then I thought if going to church is like this, I am not going to church any more.

As you can expect, it did not help our marriage because God was not in our home nor was His word being read as much, we were in trouble. I decided to get in a band and use my musical talents that way. I played drums, bass guitar but was best at playing guitar. I thought if I could get with a band, I could make more money than I did at work.

My plan was to keep my job but play with the band on the side and forget about church and gospel music and go into country music where I thought I could make a good living.

I finally got in with a country group called "Sue and the Hitchhikers." I know the name may sound strange but the group was actually quite good. They wanted to play in nightclubs so we practiced day and night until we felt ready. I had to decide if I was going to play in the clubs or not.

I struggled over it in my spirit because I had been and taught that it was wrong. I didn't know whether to do it or not but since I was away from God and His church, I decided it was the only thing I could do.

See how the devil can convince you of things that are not true? It was not the only thing I could do, but I convinced myself it was. I went on playing and writing country music and I was quite good at it. When we played in bars they paid us very well.

"Wow, I should have been doing this a long time ago." I thought. But, you see, I used the money for the wrong purpose, didn't put it to use for God. Instead, I used it for the devil by trying to get fame for myself.

One night when we were playing in a bar, I sang a song I had written named "Nobody Loves Here Anymore." A lady at the bar heard it and really liked it. She came up to the band afterwards and asked who wrote that song. I told her I was the writer. "I know someone you need to see in Nashville," she said. I will come and introduce you to them personally. Have you ever heard of Lynn Anderson?"

"Oh, yes," I said. "The lady who sings, "I Never Promised You A Rose Garden?" "Yes," she said. "She's becoming very popular, very famous right now. Her mother and father have a company called A Team Enterprises where they have their own writers and sign contracts with people to be writers. The songwriters' receive royalties for successful songs they write. You need to talk to these people and let them hear your song."

I was all excited about it so I packed my bags and made my way to Nashville, Tennessee where I met Casey and Elizabeth; Lynn Anderson's parents and owners of A Team Enterprises. They were so impressed by some of the songs I had written that they were willing to sign a five-year contract with me to be a writer. I was just beside myself! This had been the dream of my life. I could do something I enjoyed, have money and not be controlled by others the way I had most of my life.

I signed the contract, worked hard at writing songs and spent a lot of time in Nashville trying to develop new styles of country music. I was trying to come up with new ideas, tricky statements and phrases that would go over well on the market. They accepted several of my songs to be recorded in their studio. I demoed the songs for some of the finest musicians in Nashville who then recorded them to be "pitched" to the stars.

I wrote a song called "Why Did He Have to Pick My Rose." Mo Bandy liked it and wanted to put in on the cover of one of his albums. I thought, "I am on my way just think of it! I can have some money now and fame. I can be recognized and the world will know who I am now." Yes, fame, the devil's spotlight.

Later I realized another word that goes with fame is pride. Sometimes I wonder if we should use the word pride instead of fame. I was so caught up with myself that I was taking my recordings to all of my friends and said, "Look what I have accomplished. Look what I have done and listen, can you believe I wrote this?"

The songs were good, so good that they were going to be recorded by a star. I knew that a large sum of money was on its way. I was told that it was just a matter of time now, all I had to do was sign a release for this song. I could hardly wait.

Then one night everybody in the studio had gone so I was there by myself. I take that back, I didn't know it but angels and God were there with me too. I sat in the chair looking at the walls in the room. I saw the piano, the horns, the organ, the guitars and my guitar then all at once something came back to my memory. "This sure doesn't look like the church I used to go to." I looked it over and thought, "God, I miss being with You and the Bible studies. I miss the words that thrilled my heart and brought peace to my soul. I miss it Lord, I miss it. I'm sorry Lord, and if I am doing wrong, help me. Maybe if I make some money then I can do something for You, God." It really wasn't a foolish prayer.

All at once something deep inside me was hurting, aching, longing for the presence of God. I don't know if you have ever had that aching from needing the presence of God when He is not there but it's the most terrible feeling you can have, being separated from God's presence. I knew I was not where I should be with God and while sitting there quiet, I heard something in my heart say, "By thy words thou shall be justified and by thy words thou shall be condemned." Then I heard, "Every idle word that men shall speak they shall give an account there of in the Day of Judgment." You know that came back to me. I never memorized that scripture, it just came back to me in the Spirit of the Living God. I never really grasped and understood what it meant until that moment. God was saying to me that the music might be beautiful, I might have a talent for writing and I might even be able to reach the world, but what is the message behind the words of my songs?

People want to party, drink and do things that the Lord says is not right. If you are going to be successful in the entertainment world you have to keep up with the trend. They wanted me to write songs that would keep people drinking in the bars and committing adultery; songs that would make people think doing wrong is okay.

"What are the words you are giving people?" God said. "The words you are giving them are words you are going to be accountable for. You are going to give an account for the message you are giving the people."

I didn't know what to say, how to respond to God's words and didn't know how to make any of my songs good anymore. For the first time, I saw my pride.

Suddenly, I didn't seem so big anymore. I became humble and said, "I'm sorry, God. I'm so sorry. From this day forward I will write nothing more but words that will glorify you" and

I meant it too. I got up from that chair and to this day, as I write these words, I have never written another song unless it had to do with God. He knows that and He knows my heart. I realized this is what really matters so I told the people at A Team Enterprise I would not be signing the contract.

You would not believe their reaction. My goodness, they thought they were going to lose money and told me what a fool I was to lose all the money I would have received; a greater sum of money than I could have ever had in my life. But, you know, it didn't matter anymore, I cared more that what I was doing was morally right than I did about having personal financial gain.

I walked away and at last I felt clean, pure, and right with God. I quit writing country songs and started writing gospel music for the Master. Every song I have written since that day, are songs I can sing knowing in my heart that I am singing songs that are right and will bless, bring health and peace and I am not at all ashamed of that to this very day.

> Art thou called being a servant? Care not for it: but if thou mayest be made free, us it rather. (22) For he that is called in the Lord, being a servant, is the Lord's freeman: likewise also he that is called, being free, is Christ's servant.
> 1 Corinthians 7:21-22

Chapter 15

THE WRECK AND THE RESURRECTION

Be sober, be vigilant; because your adversary the devil, as a roaring lion, walketh about, seeking whom he may devour. (9) Whom resist stedfast in the faith, knowing that the same afflictions are accomplished in your brethren that are in the world. (10) But the God of all grace who hath called us unto his eternal glory by Christ Jesus, after that ye have suffered a while, make you perfect, stablish, strengthen, settle you.
1 Peter 5:8-10

I WOULD BE SAFE in saying that this is probably the most powerful section of my book. I am going to tell you things that happened to me in this chapter you might have a hard time believing. It is true and as a reader, you are going to have to trust me in this.

I had returned from Nashville after giving up the job writing for A Team Enterprises. Things were not going the way I thought they would and I wasn't doing well financially but I was very pleased with the way things were going with

God. I was going to go all out writing for God if it made money or not. Of course, anytime you decide to go into a ministry doing something for God, the enemy is right around the corner. I never dreamed in a million years I would get attacked like this.

I had a friend; Billy, who worked with me at Holly Carburetor and we decided to take a ride in his car and have a good time driving around. We were on a four-lane highway, two lanes on each side with a median in between. We were in the left lane to turn left at the intersection going to a trailer park to visit some friends. When we stopped to wait for the cars coming out and cars in the other lanes to clear the intersection, a man coming from behind us was going very fast. We were not warned and he never hit his brakes. He kept coming and BAM, he hit us. It knocked the car across the median, the other two lanes and into the ditch. It hit us from the back on the passenger side and we didn't have time to even think about what was happening.

The man who hit us had been drinking, was totally drunk and we don't know if he even saw us, but he was not injured. Billy was sore in his back and arms but was not badly injured. I was a little sore in my back and neck but I felt okay. I got out of the car and kind of shook my head to clear it a little bit. The police came and asked if we would like to go to the hospital to be checked out. He felt that we should but I didn't want to because I felt fine.

We had someone come pick us up because the car could not be driven. Billy was worried about his car and how to explain the situation to his wife. I went home and as I started up the steps, something was wrong, the room started to spin, my head felt funny and I was sick to my stomach. I didn't know what in the world was happening and fell to my knees. I was trying to stand but I didn't have any strength, something physically was wrong. I fell to the floor then my wife and friends who were there tried to help me. They rushed me to the emergency room where they ran several tests. They asked me to come back the next day when the test results would be in and said I could go home.

I was in bed all night, could not get up and walk. I was in such pain I cannot explain it. The pain was coming from my neck and my back and my ears were ringing and hurting. I just didn't know what it was.

When I returned to the emergency room to get the results of my tests, they decided to admit me to the hospital because they could not determine what was causing my pain. They ran more tests and took x rays but of course, I was no better. They even had thoughts I might be faking the pain. Finally, after a long search, they found in a neck x ray that it was cracked. If you know anything about neck injuries, you know they can be very serious. Your central nervous system is in the center of the neck and mine had been badly damaged. It caused ringing in the ears and the doctor said the nerves to my ears had been crushed and would deteriorate. He said it is doubtful the ringing could be stopped without clipping the nerve which would also result in leaving me deaf. He did not want to do that unless it was absolutely necessary to keep me from going out of my mind because of the pain and ringing. That is what I was facing. I was put in traction in the hospital for several months.

The pain did not quit nor did the ringing. I began to lose weight because I could not eat. I weigh 190 pounds today but when I lost all that weight in the hospital, I weighed only 91 pounds. I was half the person I am today, just dwindling away, literally dying. I remember the look on the doctors' faces when they were doing all they could do, but even so, I was dying.

They decided I might as well be at home where I wanted to be and would be more comfortable.

I stayed in bed, not being able to walk or do anything. Someone else was feeding me and someone else had to take care of me for one year. Yes, one year. My body had become so weak and so frail that I had become totally dependent on others to take care of me.

Let me back up for just a moment because we are going to get into something so powerful that I don't want to leave it out. Let me say this, in the middle of this tragedy, the devil brought another tragedy into my life even more terrible. Now what in the world could be worse than knowing I am about to die. Well, there was something worse.

The doctors had diagnosed me and could not give a certain time but they knew if I continued this way, I was going to die. When they sent me home from the hospital, I was in traction every day and could only have it removed at night while I slept. I was in constant pain all day and the many medications they tried did not make it stop. It was so horrible I wanted to die. Death seemed better to me than this kind of *life*. I was lying there suffering and Elizabeth could not handle it so she invited her sister to come visit us. She felt having some of her family with her would help with the stress she was having but when her sister came, she tried to convince my wife to leave me.

My mother did not live too far from us and she came by to see me on her way to work. My sister-in-law told Elizabeth my mother could take care of me, that she didn't need this burden on her and I was going to die anyway.

Elizabeth packed her bags while I was lying in bed and there was nothing I could do. I just couldn't believe it and I was in so much pain which was more concerning than anything. But then, even worse, Tausha and Jeremy ran to me and held onto my bed. They had heard my wife and her sister talking and realized they were leaving for good but they didn't want to leave me. They were holding on to the side of the bed saying, "Daddy, we don't want to go. Daddy! Daddy! don't make us go." To this day when I hear a little child cry out for daddy, my heart falls within me.

The physical pain I had was horrible but not as horrible as this pain. The worst part of it all was there was nothing I could do. I could not stand on my feet to reach out, grab my kids and hold onto them. I lay there helpless in traction and I will never forget the agony and pain as I heard the door shut. I was still hearing my kids crying and saying, "Daddy!" The sound of their voices grew fainter and fainter as they got in the car. At that moment, I thought for sure I was going to go out of my mind, I could not cope with anything. All I wanted to do right then was die. I remember my prayer was, "God, why don't You just let me die?" But God was not going to let me die, He had a purpose and a plan. Although I could not understand it at the time.

Needless to say, I got much worse, even to the point I could not operate parts of my body. I was rushed back to the hospital and I knew the time was coming when I was going to die. While there my heart began to pound so hard and fast, and because of my blood pressure, I was going to die. Right then they carried me into a room and left me. It was like isolation and they would not allow anyone in.

As I lay there with my heart pounding so hard, I was weakening but knew I was ready to go. As I went, the first thing I saw was darkness. I want you to understand, I am not talking about like when you close your eyes and see dark. This darkness was the darkest I have ever seen. Black velvet is dark but black velvet would have been pale compared to the darkness I saw. In this darkness I could feel myself being pulled as if I was going somewhere. Even though I could not see, I knew I was moving. It felt as if I was going upward. I couldn't tell if I was going fast or slow, if that makes any sense, but that was exactly what was happening.

Suddenly it seemed as if I stopped in mid-air. There were no boundaries around me of any kind and was as if a person could stand in the middle of the air. I tried to look with my eyes but there was nothing to see because it was so black. Suddenly the blackness began to pale or become lighter and continued to lighten until it turned into a grayish, bluish color. As that grayish, bluish color came, I saw it was a horse as large as the world I was in. It was passing me by right before my eyes. The horse was so large I could not see all of it. This grayish, bluish color was just passing by and I had no idea what it meant. Now that I look back and have prayed, read the word of God and studied about it, I feel like it had something to do with the angel of death passing by. God had to bring me into a dimension of death to show me what He was going to reveal to me next.

It passed by not touching me and yet I was brought into another dimension. As it passed by I saw a light, a light yellowish color and it was standing in mid-air. I moved my hands and feet and if I turned to the right I went right and if I turned to the left I went left. I had full control of gravity. As I was standing there in mi-air, I looked around and saw far off it looked as if there was some sort of cloud or mist, if you want to call it that. It was rising up to a certain extent and was a whitish-looking color coming up.

I could see there were people on the other side. I could not make out their faces and could not tell you what they looked like since it was at such a distance, but they were people for sure. They looked as if they were wearing robes and seemed to be in the yellowish light and the white rising mist that was coming up from underneath. The people stayed with it as it rose. It looked as though there was a great, great multitude. I was seeing only the tip, like the beginning of it. Then in the background I noticed above them what appeared to be angelic beings but I could not make them out completely.

As I saw this from afar trying to see it all, I realized I was standing somewhere in the middle between earth and heaven. I could not be in heaven and I could not be on earth. Then I heard a voice, and when I heard this voice, I knew what John meant when he said, "Like the voice of many waters." I had never heard a voice like it. It was so awesome that it shook my very being. It began to speak and said, "Have you not spoken the words that I have given you? Have I not called you to preach the gospel?" Oh my God! I knew what He meant was that He had called me to preach and I was running, running so hard. I didn't want to preach the gospel, didn't want to be a preacher. Thank God I remember this one thing, I needed to repent. I cried out to God in great desperation. "Lord, You know if you will forgive me, if you will give me another chance, I will preach the gospel." I just cried out to Him. I was very aware that He knew my heart and that I meant it. I wondered as I finished praying what God was going to do with me. Was I going to go on to heaven now or, because I had disobeyed God, was I going to hell? Was I going back to earth? What is God going to do with me?

I stood there in silence, total complete silence. I realized God was going to do something. Suddenly that same yellow light I had seen began to get dimmer and dimmer. The same bluish color began to come into that color. I felt as if I was passing through some transformation and was going back from where

I came. The next thing I remember was that my eyes were opening and was back in the room I had left. I looked around me. I thought, I have had an experience with God! I know many people will say it was the medicine, a hallucination or something else but it was not any of that. How was I going to convince anyone this really did happen? Then I realized I didn't have to do that, I only had to do what God told me to do, preach the gospel. How was I going to do that? I was bed fast lying there in this affliction, still not well. The devil tried to make me doubt by asking, "How could you have an encounter with God and come back sick?" And I *was* still sick.

They moved me back into my room and was beginning to get a little better. I was still in pain and had the same symptoms but wasn't quite as bad as before. Some of it had been taken away, enough so that I could now talk. I could tell the nurses and everyone what I saw, about the experience I had. Of course they all looked at me like I was silly and didn't know what I was talking about. Let me tell you, that was a terrible feeling to have an experience like that and people didn't want to hear about it when I knew how real it was.

When I was released from the hospital, I had a friend who took me into her home feeding me and helping all she could to get me back on my feet. I was still bed fast and when I tried to stand on my feet I became limp. I had no equilibrium, could not function or do work of any kind. I had to deal with that day and night, trying to stand on my feet and not able to. I did not know what I was going to do. The pain wasn't as severe as before, but I still could not do anything with my body.

I prayed and asked the Lord to help me. I came to the point that I knew the line had to be drawn. This was it, I was either going to be healed or I was going to die. I had a shoe box packed full of prescription medicine given me by the doctors and they did not work. I took the box and hit it with my arm with as much strength as I had knocking it to the floor. I told God I would not take another pill.

"God," I said. "You are going to heal me or I am going to die." The days continued on and I did not get any better. I finally told God, "I want You to give me a place where I can be alone with You and spend time with You, then just die."

A friend of the lady I was staying with, who lived across the street, came to visit saying he was going to be gone for several months and would like to find someone to stay there while he was gone.

"If they carry me over there, would you mind if I stayed in your home by myself for a little while?" I asked. "If I am going to die I could have some time alone with God."

He agreed so some of my friends helped me across the street and put me in his bed. When I was alone I thought, "This is the moment. If I am going to leave this world, let it be just God and me."

I told my friends they could come and check on me from time to time but let me have time alone with God. They did not want to do that. They were afraid to leave me because they thought I was going to die. They knew that this was something that I wanted so they finally left me there alone.

About ten o'clock that night I became more serious and desperate than I had ever been in my life. I prayed, "God, if you will help me get down on my knees I will stay there until you choose to heal me or to let me die." For some strange reason, I felt like I had to get on my knees to pray. That was so ridiculous but that is the way I had been taught. But God was hearing me all the time, God answered my prayers and I was given strength in my body to move to the edge of the bed. Then I put my feet over and slid down the side of the bed to the floor. That made me so happy, even though I was still in terrible pain. When I got on my knees I stayed there and prayed for a very long time. When my vocabulary ended and there was nothing more I could say or do, I felt as if I was going to stay there and die.

All at once a light came in that room, the most beautiful light I had ever seen. Don't ask me to explain it because it cannot be explained. The only way I can try to describe it is as a light inside a light. It was different shades of light, but it was light. I would call it the glory of God that came into that room. I saw it with my physical eye, not my spiritual eye. It filled the room completely and when it hit me something happened. Suddenly I noticed my ears were not ringing, I mean no ringing. That ringing was with me for one year and now there was no ringing. I was so amazed by this I shook my head in disbelief when I realized my body was not in pain. I had no pain, my arms were moving, my legs were moving and I had strength in them.

I stood to my feet and the light was still in the room. The first thing I said was, "My God! I am healed!" Then I shouted a while, praised a while and glorified God. Then I knew I had to tell someone, do something. I got dressed as fast as I could, went outside and walked across the street.

Think about this. You cannot lie in a bed for a full year then be able to get up and just take off! I tell you, with God as my witness, that is exactly what I did! I walked across to the lady's house where she had taken care of me and knocked on the door. She opened the door and saw me, I thought her eyes were going to pop out of their sockets. She was so shocked she put her hand over her mouth and said nothing. She could not speak.

"The Lord has healed me!" I said. "You're healed?" she

asked. "Yes," I said. "God has healed me and called me to preach the gospel. You are the first one I have told about it."

When God comes on the scene, He will give you a testimony that will bless everyone around you. He is a God full of blessings. The wool was pulled from my eyes at that moment allowing me to see that God is still a healer. You cannot convince me by any means that God does not heal. He is the same as He was when he walked in Galilee and healed the sick, the lame, the blind and the deaf. Friends, He is the same God!

> *Surely he hath borne our griefs, and carried our sorrows: yet we did esteem him stricken, smitten of God, and afflicted. (5) But he was wounded for our transgressions, he was bruised for our iniquities: the chastisement of our peace was upon him: and with his stripes we are healed.*
> Isaiah 53:4-5

Chapter 16

PURIFICATION AND THE POWER TO PREACH

For though I preach the gospel, I have nothing to glory of, for necessity is laid upon me, yea, woe is unto me, if I preach not the gospel.
1 Corinthians 9:16

AT THIS TIME I was so worked up an army of men could not have been kept me from preaching. I was going to preach the gospel if I had to walk out in the middle of the street. Whatever I had to do, I was going to preach the gospel. I called a friend of mine who was the pastor of a church I had attended and told him what had happened. It was so hard for him to believe because he knew the physical condition I was in. I went to talk to him and he said, "You can come to our church next Sunday and preach a message."

I thought, my God, I am going to preach a message. It suddenly hit me that I did not know how to preach. I realized I did not know enough scriptures and had never stood before a group of people and given a message. I knew I was not prepared and if God did not help me I could not do it. I began to study my Bible and prayed asking God to help me. I remember staying up half the night worrying, yes worrying, because I didn't trust God. Can you believe that? He healed me divinely, supernaturally, and I couldn't trust Him to help me preach the Word. Isn't that ridiculous? I stayed up half the night worrying about this message. I studied with everything I had and then thought I was ready. I prayed everything I could pray and then when it came time to preach that Sunday morning, when I got behind the pulpit, I read the title of the message I had prepared for and the Holy Spirit spoke to my soul. He said, "Don't preach on that; preach on this." "Oh my God!" I thought. "Lord, I know nothing about that. This is what I studied all night."

The Lord began to reveal to me to speak on what He told me to speak on. I was determined that I heard from God so I spoke on what He told me to speak on. When I did, the Holy Spirit came upon me and took control of my message and I said the words the Lord wanted me to say. Several people at that service got saved. Some people got healed and some people fell in the Spirit. Powerful things happened at church that Sunday, things they had not seen in a very long time.

I began to see that it is not through knowledge or wisdom, but "By My Spirit saith the Lord." We don't have the might and we don't have the strength but when it comes to preaching the gospel we must learn how to follow the leadership of the Holy Spirit. God had to bring purification inside of me. He had to start purifying and emptying me of the things that kept me from doing and saying what He wanted me to do and say. It took that for me to be ready to preach the gospel with the power of the Holy Ghost.

God had many things to teach me before I came to that place. Even today He is still working to purify me and sift me through the sifter so I will be willing to do what He wants me to do and say.

Let me say something to you about what the Lord revealed to me. I asked the Lord in prayer one time, "What is a preacher?" Now that I was going to preach the gospel, I wanted to know the definition of a preacher, what a preacher is exactly.

I have been told that a preacher is someone in the church who is respected who will bring forth the word of God, a man who is called of God to speak for God. I have been told we can all preach but that doesn't mean we are all called to be ministers or pastors. We all have a message given to us by God, but what is a preacher?

It was awesome what the Lord told me. I have heard many things about what a preacher is but I have never heard it put this way. The Lord spoke to me and said, "A preacher is nothing more than a channel where My heart can touch his heart, where it can touch people's hearts."

When I took a good look at that, I realized God has something He wants to say. A preacher is a man who will preach what God tells him to preach. If a man has it all figured out, it is not of God. God began to reveal to me there were things that had to be weeded out of my life so that I would be willing to go where He wants me to go and say what He tells me to say. If I could do that, He would take care of the rest and my ministry would be successful. After that, there were several churches where I was privileged to preach. Many years passed by, I saw many good revivals and I was learning many things.

I was learning about all the gifts of the Spirit; the word of wisdom, the word of knowledge, faith, gifts of healing, the working of miracles, prophecy, the discerning of spirits, the gift of tongues and the interpretation of tongues. You will find these nine gifts mentioned in the book of I Corinthians chapter

12. I was also learning about the fruit of the Spirit and things in the Bible I had not been taught in church.

I learned about the supernatural power of God that is available to people today who are willing to seek His face, understand and receive that power. The more I learned and the more I searched, the more I could see that most of us have not really hungered and thirsted for God the way we should. The Bible says if we hunger and thirst after Him we will be filled and I believe our hungering and thirsting is not to the place it really needs to be. God was bringing me to that place. I felt I had learned about His gifts and several of them were beginning to operate in my life. The gift of healing being one of them when my body was miraculously healed. I saw God wanted me to do greater things than I was doing.

Then God opened up something for me I had always wanted to do. I have already told you I am a singer and musician but I came across some people who were starting a gospel band. I was the lead guitar player and we had a drummer, a rhythm guitar player, a bass player, a lead singer and some back-up singers. It was really a wonderful gospel band and I had the privilege of naming the band "The Redemptions." We had plans to travel, sing gospel songs in churches where the Spirit of God could come and there would be an atmosphere for the people to be blessed.

God was blessing us greatly and as doors opened for us to sing, we entered and were having a wonderful time traveling and singing. It was some of the best times I ever had in my life. I really enjoyed singing and being with people, hearing the ways they believed, being in their churches and just associating with them. I think God gave me this opportunity because I was learning how people in other religions believed. We did not prevent ourselves from going to any church regardless of their religion. We were just singing the gospel and letting God move and do what He wanted to do. This also gave me a wonderful opportunity to preach the gospel. Some of the churches limited our time and others gave us a lot of time to sing. That gave me a chance to give my testimony and preach a little while even though we did not have the entire service. That really blessed and helped me.

I saw so many wonderful things happen as I played and sang with this band. I would like to share one special thing that touched my heart and has stayed with me through the years. We visited a church in Bowling Green, Kentucky but I would rather not name the church or it's denomination. Our group began to sing and all at once the Lord impressed upon my heart to have every musician lay their instruments down on the floor. Now to me that sounded utterly ridiculous and couldn't understand why the Lord would want us to do such a thing. It just seemed crazy to do this here in front of everybody in this church where we traveled many miles to sing. We had practiced our music, but the Lord said, "Tell your musicians to lay their instruments on the floor."

Everyone in our group really loved God so I got bold. They had heard me preach enough that they knew if the Lord told me to do something, He was going to do something.

I turned to them and said, "The Lord said to take off our instruments and lay them on the floor." They looked at me a little weird and the congregation looked at me weird but we laid our instruments on the floor. I began to tell of my experience, how the Lord had healed me. The Lord really moved upon my heart because He really wanted me to tell how He healed me. The tears flowed down my face as the Spirit of God helped me tell my story. I knew there was some divine reason but I did not understand why God wanted me to testify.

Suddenly an elderly lady in the middle of the congregation was crying as she stood up. Then some of the other members of the congregation began to stand up. They were no doubt touched by the story of how the Lord had healed me. I didn't know if they wanted to testify or just what the Lord wanted. Then I saw they were wanting to be prayed for so I turned and looked at the pastor. We had come to sing and I didn't want to take over the service. This was his congregation and I didn't know what they believed or what they didn't believe.

I noticed as I was talking, the preacher was looking at me strangely, staring a hole right through me. I found out later that this church did not believe in healing, did not believe in the supernatural power of God or the gifts of the Holy Spirit. They believed in the Holy Ghost but for some reason they didn't believe in the gifts of the Spirit, the laying on of hands when praying for someone sick nor the supernatural healing power of the Lord.

Since they did not believe these things, my story probably seemed rather ridiculous to the pastor. He evidently thought it was not the Lord who had healed me. I don't know what was going through his mind or that this church did not believe in this, I was just obeying God.

All at once this lady who had stood up first began to walk down the aisle. She came to the front, looked at me and said, "Would you please pray for me? I have something that I really need someone to help me pray for."

"We will be glad to pray for you," I said. Now this little group of good musicians, "The Redemption" were praying people, believe me and they were sitting on ready. We were wondering if we needed the pastor's approval or what when this little lady looked at me and said, "I have a grandson who is in the hospital right now and they really don't know if he will live. He has been in the hospital for about three months and is the only grandchild I have. Would you please pray for him? I don't want to lose him."

As she looked at me, I suddenly realized what God was doing. There were people here who needed to be ministered to more than just having a song sung to them. They were in desperate need of healing. Their church did not teach it and evidently they never got to hear about the working of miracles and the gift of healing. They knew that God heals but did not know where to go or what to do to receive this healing.

She came standing before me and said, "Your testimony really touched my heart and maybe you can help me pray for my grandson."

The pastor gave me that look again but I wanted to obey God, even if they threw me out of the church. I knew our group believed the Bible and in laying on of hands as the Bible says so I asked the group to come gather around this lady. You see that is why God had all of us lay our instruments on the floor. He wanted us to agree in prayer and be able to lay our hands on this lady.

We laid our hands on her and began to pray for her grandson then she went back to her seat. I could see the pastor was getting a little upset but he came over and he allowed us to sing just a few songs. I think he wanted us to quickly end this service. Afterwards he gave his message and then we came back up and sang a couple of songs. As we sang, the Spirit of the Lord began to get us into a state of worship. I could tell this church was not used to praise and worship nor had they entered into that realm of worship when they could feel the closeness of God. We began to play and sing and the Spirit moved so sweetly. It seemed I could not play my guitar anymore so I just sang before the Lord, and oh my God, I did something else that was probably not accepted in the church.

I began to sing in the Spirit, to let the Spirit take control, singing and looking to God. I did not know what song we were singing any more, I just lost it and knew I was singing to Jesus, of how much I loved Him. I was just saying the most beautiful things to Him because you know I do that sometimes.

When I got through singing the song and things quieted down, I opened my eyes and looked at the people in the congregation. There were tears in everyone's eyes and I saw they were experiencing something they had never experienced before. The pastor said it was time to close the service but one lady asked him to let us sing one more song. The pastor said that time was running out but she said, "Please, will you let them sing one more song?"

We began to sing again and then the Spirit of praise and worship did enter there and we sang one of the songs we knew well. They enjoyed it so much and we got a wonderful applause. We just had the most wonderful time and after that, the pastor closed the service.

We went down to the basement where they were preparing a dinner that day for a special event they were having. They were having a huge meal and invited us all to come and eat before we left. I tell you what, the group I was with loved to eat, so we stayed for a meal. The pastor asked the blessing on the food and we sat down at tables to eat. We sat around the table enjoying our food and having a wonderful time then I noticed the lady who had asked us to pray with her for her grandson. She looked so sad sitting at the end of the table by herself. It seemed strange to me that none of the ladies in the church were associating with her. I didn't know the reason why and didn't want to get involved so I just sat and watched. I thought maybe they were a little offended by her asking for prayer and they thought it was not the way the pastor believed. It was not how they had been taught so they just drifted from her a little bit.

While sitting there eating, something incredible happened. We heard a knock at the door at the top of the stairs where we had gone down to the basement and one of the ladies of the church ran up to open the door. There stood a man in a white outfit, something like a hospital worker might wear. He asked for the lady whose grandson we prayed for. I thought maybe someone had come to visit her and everyone watched as he came down the steps. He was an aide at the hospital where her grandson was and told the lady he had good news. He lived down the road and was told the little boy's grandmother would be at a dinner at the church. He didn't want her to have to wait until she got home to hear the good news.

Her eyes lit up and she asked, "Is he better? Is my grand baby better?" The aid looked at her and said, "No, your grand baby is not better, your grand baby is well! He has been struggling for his life all the time he has been in the hospital and we did not know if he would survive. About thirty minutes ago we could tell by the baby's crying something is different. His lungs sounded stronger and he was like a different baby."

He said the nurse contacted the doctor because she thought something was wrong. The baby was hooked up to several tubes, etc. and the doctor came in to check him. When the doctor checked the baby and listened to his heart he said, "This baby's heart is beating correctly. I don't understand." The doctor quickly ordered an x-ray so they could look closely at the baby's heart. When the doctor looked at the x-rays he called in some of his associates who examined them as well and said the hole that had been in the baby's heart was not there anymore.

The hospital aide said, "I know some doctors don't believe in this kind of thing happening and say it must have a medical explanation." "But these are my friends I work with and they saw this. Your grand-baby's heart is well and he will be going home any time you want to pick him up."

"Oh, God," I thought. "You even sent somebody to the door to give a witness to this church needing it so desperately for them to know that You still heal supernaturally, so they would know that the laying on of hands, praying with faith, believing, touching and agreeing does work. Maybe you will see it happening in this church after we leave."

That Grandmother was the happiest woman you have ever seen. She didn't care if nobody would associate with her, she shot out of that church like a rocket. I knew where she was going, she was going to get that grand baby and it really touched my heart. Sometimes we have this "plan" thinking we need to go somewhere and sing, but God can interrupt our "plans" and we can see wonderful things happen as we obey and do what He tells us to.

One other event I want to tell you about is the first miracle I experienced in my ministry and is one of the greatest miracles I have ever experienced. You may think it sounds unbelievable, or too good to be true, but I assure you it did happen.

I had taken off work to do some much needed things at home. I called work and my foreman said it was okay for me to be off a couple of days. I was thankful I had been allowed time off to get those important things done. When I woke up the next morning to go back to work, the Lord spoke to me saying "Don't go to work." Oh no I thought.

"I'll lose my job. I can't do this." The Lord told me, "I want you to pray." I got down on my knees and began to pray. Then the Lord said, "I want you to call Barbara because she needs your prayers."

I wondered why in the world God wanted me to call Barbara, a lady I worked with. She and I were machine operators at Holly Carburetor. I did not have her phone number but knew the Lord wanted me to call her so I looked up her number and called. Her daughter answered and I asked for Barbara. She asked who I was and I'm sure she wondered why I wanted to talk to her mother. I just said I needed to talk to Barbara, not knowing exactly what about. I know that sounds ridiculous but that is the way the Lord works sometimes.

Her daughter told me Barbara was not there. "Where is she?" I asked. She said "She is in the hospital and is very bad, haven't you heard?"

"Oh, no," I said. "No, I've been off work for a couple days. What's wrong with her?" "Oh, Glen!" she said. "Mom's got cancer and it's really bad." We'll pray, don't worry, Barbara is going to be okay." I said. "I don't know Glen, I've never seen Mom this bad," she said.

Barbara had been a gospel singer and sung gospel music in churches in the area. She was a wonderful singer and loved the Lord but had been offended by someone in one of those churches and she even stopped going to church. Then she got this terrible disease; cancer, and the Lord really impressed on my heart to go to the hospital and pray for her. I thought, oh no, I can't take another day off of work, I may get fired.

You know how all those things go through your mind. I made up my mind that I was going to obey the Lord so I called in to work and told my boss that I needed one more day off. I knew he was going to get upset. "Is it very important?" he asked. I said it was very important and "You know Barbara is in the hospital and I want to visit her. I just want to go see her."

"Oh, yes," he said. "You go ahead and take off another day." This man never does this. If you know about foremen, this man was Mr. Iron pants, never letting anybody off. But you know, God intended for this to happen.

I went to the hospital and walked into Barbara's room. Oh, my God, I could sense and the presence of death in that room and I could not believe the way she looked after not having seen her for only three days. She was in much pain and they had her drugged so much I could see the darkness under her eyes, all the worry and fear she had. Evidently they had told her how bad the cancer was.

I walked up to her and her gown was pulled down on one side where the cancer was. There was a hole in her shoulder that was black and terrible looking. I mean it was literally like a large hole. I thought this woman must have had this a long time and suffered with it, not telling anyone and then it got extremely worse.

As she was lying there I looked at her and said, "Barbara, this morning the Lord told me not to go to work but instead to call you."

The tears began to flow from her eyes and she said, "Glen, this morning I prayed with everything in me but I don't have the strength to pray. I'm so weak I can hardly talk and I prayed for God to send somebody to come help me pray. None of my family, except my daughter, has been here and she hasn't stayed very long. Would you please pray for me, help me?"

I have never been so touched in all my life. Yes, I had been called to preach the gospel and this was my opportunity to do what God called me to do, to help people, bless people, to command blessings upon them, but this woman was dying.

How do I do that? God is showing me about a new level of faith. I remember thinking not to worry or be afraid. Sometimes you have those concerns about cancer.

I took my hand and laid it right on top of that cancerous spot. I knew it hurt her even though I laid it on her very lightly. I began to pray and at the time, I felt my prayer was going no higher than the ceiling. I don't know why but I felt like something was restraining me, like the presence of death. I had experienced that when I was dying but not when being in the room with someone else who was dying. With my hand on her shoulder, I began to pray asking the Lord to heal her, restore her and make her completely whole.

"I leave this in the hands of the Lord," I said. I prayed but as far as feeling, I felt like it was dead but I kept trusting what the Word says and speaking it until I was exhausted with my prayer. I looked at Barbara and said, "Barbara, don't worry. God is going to take care of you." A big smile came to her face.

She was too weak to talk, too weak to do anything and she closed her eyes. I didn't know if she was dying or what was happening but I knew it was time for me to go. I walked out of her room and the devil was trying to tell me, "Your prayer didn't get anywhere, you think you are so powerful. You have been preaching about your supernatural healing, heal this woman? She is dying!"

Something just swelled up in me and the Holy Spirit started convincing me, "You don't have to take that, only believe!" I began to believe beyond the natural that Barbara was going to be ok. So I left her room and went home then back to work.

Friend, like I said, it sounds unbelievable but with God as my witness, this happened. The next evening when I was at

K-Mart, I turned down an aisle and guess who was standing in front of me, Barbara! She was out of the hospital! When I first got a glimpse of her I wondered if that could really be Barbara.

When she turned and saw me, she just hollered really loud, "Glen!" She came running and put her arms around me and started shouting really loud, "Praise the Lord! Praise the Lord! Glory to God!" I mean she was getting loud right there in K-Mart.

"How in the world did you get out of the hospital?" I asked. Friend, this is the truth I'm giving you. She pulled her blouse down over her shoulder and the cancer was all dried up, the hole that was black, the most awful thing I had seen in my life, looked as if it had been covered with dry skin. It was just drying completely up. This happened in just a few hours.

She said, "The doctor came in, looked at the cancer and said it was just remarkable." He said he knew some of the things they used and radiation had all helped, but he had never seen anything like this. He even wrote on her report that he had never seen anything like it and that he did not know what had caused her to heal the way she did.

She looked at me and said, "Isn't this a miracle?"

"Oh, glory to God!" I said. "This is a miracle, a wonderful, supernatural miracle! Barbara, what are you going to do with this? Why don't you get back in church and start singing for Jesus again? Tell people about this!"

I saw a tear come down her cheek and she said, "Glen, you are right. That is what I really need to be doing. I got away from God and the devil was putting a lot of things in my way trying to hinder me. I allowed him to do that, I gave up but not anymore. I'm going to go back to singing for Jesus. This has changed my life."

That is the last time I saw her. I believe with all my heart that because of the faith in God's word and believing what He says is true caused Barbara to be healed, not lying in bed taking shots, suffering the rest of her life or maybe even dead. God can heal you instantaneously. I believe God revealed that to me at the first healing; the first person for me to pray for, to show me, encourage and convince me that the ministry I was going to be would involve healing. Yes, He wants me to be involved in a healing ministry. Even though he had miraculously healed me, I didn't know that He wanted me to be in the healing ministry. I thought He wanted me to go out singing and preaching the gospel. I believe He caused this miraculous healing so quickly because He wanted me to see this was an area He wanted included in my ministry, the gift of healing.

> *But the manifestation of the spirit is given to every man to profit withal. (8) For to one is given by the spirit the word of wisdom, to another the word of knowledge by the same spirit. (9) To another faith by the same spirit, to another the gifts of healing by the same spirit.*
> 1 Corinthians 12:7-9

Chapter 17

NEW YORK, DEMONS AND THE OCCULT

But I say, that the things which the Gentiles sacrifice, they sacrifice to devils, and not to God. And I would not that ye should have fellowship with devils. (21) Ye cannot drink the cup of the Lord, and the cup of devils: ye cannot be partakers of the Lord's table, and of the table of the devils.
1 Corinthians 10:20-21

ONE NIGHT IN A DREAM, the Lord spoke telling me I was going to a distant land. That really confused me because I didn't know what He meant by a distant land. The devil tried to convince me this dream was not from the Lord, it was just an ordinary dream so it didn't have any real significance.

I went to church the following Sunday. Some pastors and members of our church who were dear friends of mine decided to have a revival in New York. They all came to my house after church to talk to me. They said, "Glen, we are going to have revival in New York. The door has opened for us to have a revival in Jamestown, New York and we really feel like you need to be with us and help preach some in this revival. Would you be willing to travel with us? We will pay for the trip. Will you go?"

It really amazed me and I said, "Just the other night I had a dream and the Lord told me I was going to travel to a distant land." They looked at me kind of puzzled.

The Lord had already prepared me, otherwise I would not have gone to New York for anything, there is nothing there for me. It is not my kind of place, I'm not running New York down, but that is just not where I wanted to be. The Lord wanted me to go to a distant land and now I know why He called it a distant land, it was totally and completely distant to me as I knew nothing about it at all. I am not familiar with their customs, traditions or anything. I even have a different slang than the people in New York have. Why would the Lord want me to go to New York?

You see I did not know God was bringing me to a place where I could learn things I could not learn where I was. He wanted me to go to another level to learn these things I needed to learn. Oh, but little did I know what I was about to experience and have to go through in New York.

We got there and started having a wonderful revival. I tell you what, when you preached the gospel those people got excited. When the people who were lost went to the altar, they prayed and got saved. I have never seen such a move of people praising and worshiping and wondered why there was such a great move of God in this place.

The Lord began to tell me some of these people have been through so much and are fed up with all the things they have had to go through. They have come to the place when they turn it over, they really turn it over. They have lived rough, had it hard, have seen the city life of crime and death and have seen the fear people live in. You know, when they turn it over, they turn it over. They have seen more hardships of life than people in other places I have been.

There is something else in New York I did not know about. There is a lot of Satan worship, demonology, religious cults, gangs and other things people are involved in that did not occur where I was from. There were a lot of souls saved and it was a wonderful revival.

When our revival was finished one member of another church asked us to come to his church and have services with him before we left town. "Just come visit our church," he said. We all agreed to do that to see how other churches were in that area.

That night we went out in the country to his small church and there were not very many people, maybe only twenty. We were really surprised after being in the larger church but this church was far from town. The pastor was a wonderful man of God. His name was Mr. Hallet and he preached the gospel. He was in the middle of preaching his sermon that night when he stopped and started walking toward me. This man had never met me, didn't know who I was or any of my family. I live in Kentucky, a long way from where he lives in New York.

He walked up to me and said, "The Lord is telling me that you should preach here tomorrow night."

You know that went over well. We were thinking about going back to Kentucky, I was wanting out of New York and I had already been there too long with all the demons and such.

After he spoke to me he went back up to the front and preached without asking me again if I would preach. He continued to preach a wonderful message about the attributes of the Holy Ghost. When he finished preaching, we were ready to leave and he came over and asked if I was going to come back to preach the next night.

"Oh, we have to go back to Kentucky," I answered. Then one of the ministers in our group said, "Oh, no, we don't have to go back tomorrow night." I looked at him and thought, "Oh, no, don't say that. We have to go."

But he continued, "No, we don't have to go tomorrow. We can come back tomorrow night." The pastor then asked me if I would preach the next night so I said I would. Truthfully, I didn't want to, I wanted out of that place. So we came back the next night. The Lord was opening another door for me to preach again. When I got up in the pulpit and started to preach, the Lord put a burden on my heart to preach a message on how we need to bear one another's burdens, that we need to have a greater hunger in our heart for souls and not be so interested in other things. I could see why God wanted me to preach that message because this church really needed to start doing something and build their church. The best way to build a church is to go out and try to reach people for God, be a soul winner, focusing on souls instead of trying to come up with fundraisers. You should come up with ways to invite people in so you can win them to the Lord.

There was a lot of snow in New York. I have never lived in a place where the snow was all the way up to your waist and going places was difficult. These people lived in it and were used to it but to me it was rough being where it was so cold with so much snow and I complained about it. This was just not a place I wanted to be. There were demons, snow, cold weather and a different way of life.

When I finished preaching my message, the Lord put something in my heart I don't know how to explain. What He put on my heart made me no longer care about the snow or the demons. He put something in me to let me realize these people needed me, not for what I am, but for what I have learned and experienced of Him. I needed to share these things to help them grow and to build this church. He wanted me to stay in New York where I could do the work He wanted me to do.

You know how well that went over, don't you? "Oh no God, not here, no, no" I said. Then finally I gave up and told the pastor the Lord had spoken to my heart and he said the Lord had spoken to his heart too and that he wanted to make me an assistant pastor if the church agreed. "I do need help to get my church built," he said. "You are a wonderful minister and I think the church will want you."

Of course, they voted me in so I stayed there with Brother Hallet. We alternated preaching every other week and I went around town talking to people and passing out tracts. We had singing and God used my singing talent to reach the people.

The next thing I knew more people were attending services and the church grew. I learned something I never would have if had I not stayed. I studied and learned about demons, evil spirits and about how Jesus took control over them. I studied how He commanded them to come out of people and how the evil spirits had something to do with the type of person they had become and the sicknesses they had.

I learned it wasn't the person, it was the spirit in the person causing them to be involved in the occult and other like things. Some of them had been bound so long and there was a stronghold on them. I had to learn about these spirits and try to show the people that these spirits were in them and they needed to be free of them in order to get out of the things they were involved in.

I want to tell you how dangerous it was there. A lot of people were involved in the occult, in gangs and a lot of other fearful things in that area. Through it all, God took care of me, gave me a peace, He protected me and kept me safe. He gave me knowledge and understanding about spirits. He also gave me a hunger to study about them in the Bible and how to identify them and cast them out so I could help the people.

As I studied, learned and began to grow in that area, we saw people get delivered. People lived in such fear but then they learned how to get rid of the fear. God didn't give us a spirit of fear but of power and love and a sound mind to learn these things.

Some of the people would get involved in the occult and Satan worship and sometimes the Holy Spirit would convict them and wanted to get out of that lifestyle. They saw it was wrong but once they got in so deep, some of the leaders of Satanism would come up against them and want to kill them if they gave any information about the things they knew. Some coming to our church were involved in very bad things but would come to the church and ask us to pray and help some of their friends who were also in it. Their lives were in great danger by coming to church. The Satan worshipers would sometimes spray paint a rose with black paint and lay it on their doorstep. It meant they were going to kill them or a member of their family. If you came home and found a black rose on your doorstep, that meant your life was in real danger.

Some of those people who received a black rose would run to our church if they were trying to get out of the occult. They would show us the black rose and tell us what was behind it and ask if they could stay all night at the church. We did let them stay at the church and we would stay up and pray for them all night. It was amazing how God protected them. Of course some of them did get killed but some were spared. God delivered them out of that and saved them. I thought it was so wonderful and I wish I could tell you some of their stories but that would take too long.

God was bringing me to a place where He could reveal things to me I would need to know, to operate in a ministry helping people who needed deliverance and also for me to have a greater awareness of those things in my life. I also learned about curses, signs and symbols that witches use to communicate with each other. I learned about so many things that I would never have been aware of had I not been in New York. Many of these things I learned, I taught other churches to help them recognize them and keep them away from the children and their homes. The Lord wants us to stay away from such things and be able to help people we see involved in these things and making others aware of the truth so they don't get caught up in the dangers of them putting their lives in bondage.

I stayed in New York for a year and a half then felt the Lord was finishing my ministry there. The church I was helping as assistant pastor had grown from twenty members to approximately one hundred thirty members which was a very good number for them as they were so far out into the country. God was blessing them so much with other people rising up taking positions in the church and I was so happy to see the work of the Lord established there. I really felt in my spirit that the Lord was done with me in that place but I didn't know where I was going or what I was going to do.

While I was in New York I had a job with a company that made partition walls for offices by laminating them. It was a hard job but it provided an income while I was the assistant pastor of the church. I knew the Lord was finished with me in New York but I didn't know where to go or what to do. I thought about going back to Kentucky and see if the Lord wanted me to minister there. Little did I know the next place the Lord was sending me would be a place I had prayed to find all my life. Not only that but He was sending me to a place that was going to change me like I had never been changed before.

> *How God anointed Jesus of Nazareth with the Holy Ghost and with power: who went about doing good, and healing all that were oppressed of the devil; for God was with them.*
> Acts 10:38

Chapter 18

THE REUNION OF REUNIONS

Come now, and let us reason together, saith the Lord: though your sins be as scarlet, though they be red like crimson, they shall be as wool.
Isaiah 1:18

ONE DAY as I was seeking the Lord in prayer, I was rather confused, wondering where I was going to go next. I was like most people, really low on finances and little money for travel expenses. I really felt I could not accomplish much if I had to go very far to wherever I was going. What was the Lord planning for me next? What would I do now that I am finished in New York?

The phone rang so I got up to answer it. I just could not believe who was on the other end of the phone, it was my sister who I had not seen or talked to her since I was a child. "Glen," she said. "This is your sister. You may not remember me." She told me she now lived near Palmyra, Indiana which is in the southern part of the state and is close to Corydon, the first capital of Indiana.

"I called you for a reason," she said. "What is it? Is there any way I could see or meet with you?" I asked. "We have never spent time together or gotten to know each other." "I called for another reason," she said. "I have some good news for you."

I wondered what could be better than this. I was talking to my sister and I had prayed to God for so long to help me find members of my family. I wanted to talk to them and find out what had happened to me when I was young and had been given away.

"The one who had me call you is your mother," she said. We heard from some friends that you were attending a church in Bowling Green,

Kentucky so we went to the church and talked to some people there. They told us you had gone to New York and gave us the information about the church where we might find you."

I was so excited and started thinking about seeing my mother, my real mother. I would be able to talk to her and ask questions about what had happened. Maybe I would get answers to a lot of my questions. So many things were going through my mind, including the fact that I could have a relationship with my mother and might meet some other members of my family too.

My sister and I talked for a while and she told me that she did not live too far from my mother. Any time I wanted to come visit, I could meet my mother. But there was a problem, I didn't have enough finances to go anywhere at that time.

Later I got another phone call from my sister saying she wanted to know if she could drive my mother to New York to meet me. Oh, I was really excited then so they came to New York. I don't know how to describe my excitement. So many things were going through my mind including what my mother looked like.

I want to explain to you what happened when they came to where I was. There was a little bridge across the river just before the house where I lived.

Sometimes late at night, Satan worshipers would meet under the bridge and build fires. They could be heard when they prayed to Satan and chanted to evil spirits. It was a very scary sound if you had never experienced it. As my mother and sister were coming across the bridge that night, they saw the fires and rolled the windows down. They heard the sounds and were so scared they thought about turning around and going back, even though they had traveled a great distance. Thank God they continued on to where I was staying.

I will never forget that night. There was a knock at the door and I opened it to see my sister. Then there was my mother! She opened her arms and we cried and cried as we wrapped our arms around one another. I looked at her and she looked at me. I had so many questions I wanted to ask her and we sat up almost half the night talking. She explained some things that happened when I was a child and I was so touched when I heard some of those things. Especially important was finding out the reason we got separated was not the way I had been told by others. Many of the things she told me changed my opinion about what I believed had happened. I was literally so confused wondering who was telling the truth because I had been told something different all my life. I just really believed my mother because she had come so far to see me to make things right.

My mother and sister asked me about the fires they had seen under the bridge down by the water when they were coming to my place. They said they could hear the most terrible sound they ever heard and an awful feeling something was wrong. They asked what those people were doing down there. I tried to explain the best I could, without scaring them, that people were worshiping Satan. In this particular area in New York they just do things openly and sometimes animals would even be sacrificed there. There was a meeting place for witches when they wanted to cast spells on people and such things as that.

The Satan worshipers were chanting and it was a very scary sound as they talked to demons in their language. Some of the people chant when they are communicating with Satan, especially when they are putting curses on someone to bring sickness or death to them or their family. People I have talked to who have been in the occult said they would literally quote the Bible backwards because they thought it would contradict the word of God. They knew the word of God brought blessings so they thought if they spoke it backwards it would bring curses.

My mother and sister were so scared they did not know what to do. They spent the night with me and I decided to go home with my mother and spend some time with her getting to know her.

My ministry was finished here and I felt this is what the Lord wanted me to do. This is why He reunited my mother, my sister and me. He had answered my prayers. I was going to spend time with my mother and wait to see what the Lord had planned for me to do in the future.

At about eleven o'clock that night they were getting ready for bed and there was a scrape on the window. It was like a screech across the window. My sister screamed and my mother ran into the bedroom as fast as she could and got behind the chair. My sister was lying on the couch with the cover pulled over her head, crying and they were yelling for me.

I came running from the bedroom to see what was wrong

and I heard it too. I thought, what was this? All the time I had been in New York, I was not afraid, God had given me a peace that He was taking care of me. I had walked through chain gangs, motorcycle gangs and the devil worshipers on the streets as I went back and forth to church and they did not bother me. Sometimes I know my life was in danger and people asked me how I could walk through that territory where the gangs were and not be afraid. Sometimes it would be ten or eleven o'clock at night when I walked home from church. God gave me a peace and I was not afraid. I know that it was a supernatural gift from God because any other time, I would have been afraid. God took care of me and never let anything happen to me. People were getting killed around me, and a lot of other things were happening, but I just felt totally at peace with God.

Another thing that helped me was the devil worshipers did not like to be around people who were Christians, especially ministers. They felt it took away the power they had with Satan and didn't like to be around church so they did not come around and bother me like they did others.

It was well known that I was a minister and they just didn't bother me. God made a way everywhere I went and they didn't come around me.

That night I went to the door and pulled back the curtain to look out. There was snow on the ground, maybe five or six inches, which is not a lot for New York. I was looking out the window and saw six or seven deer out there and one deer had come up to the house and had scraped its antlers against the window. They were beautiful, huge deer. I told my sister to come and look. She was afraid but I finally convinced her to look outside.

"Aren't they beautiful?" she said. "I can't believe they

come right up against the house like that." I told her they must be hungry and were looking for something to eat. I thought it was funny but it wasn't funny for my mother and sister. They spent the night and the next morning I packed everything and left with them to go to Palmyra, Indiana.

A wonderful thing happened when we got to Palmyra, I had the opportunity to meet my other two sisters. Debbie is the one who came to pick me up in New York. My other sisters are Tammy and Monica. We spent time talking and getting to know each other. I felt in some ways we were strangers. They are my sisters, but we didn't get to grow up together and I didn't see them much. It was a rather unusual situation and I found it hard to talk to them at times. I was closer to Debbie who was much friendlier and she opened her home to me more than the other two did, but I loved them all the same. We were really from two different worlds it seemed. We hadn't been raised together and it was hard to accept the fact that we were brother and sisters but I was trying to get to know them.

I spent time with my mother at her house and learned quite a few things about her. She had remarried and she and my stepfather had run a tavern, that is how people in the town knew them. My mother was a really good tap dancer when she was growing up. That is all she had known all her life. She had never been to church or had any kind of religious background. Most of our family did not go to church.

I had a chance to meet some of my uncles and aunts. It was just wonderful to make connections with my family members. I met my Uncle Roland and talked to a lot of my family for the first time. It was a wonderful reunion and I knew that this was something God had put together. It was precise timing by God and I just knew there was a divine reason for us to meet each other. I knew this was my opportunity to minister to my family. I didn't know if this would be my last chance to be with them or where God would be sending me.

I knew I needed to tell them about Jesus so I talked to every one of them about Jesus every way I could. Some of them responded to it fairly well but most of them just kind of shrugged it off and were not interested. My mother and I really discussed this matter about me being a minister. When my mother saw how dedicated I was in being a minister and preaching the gospel, she became very angry and let me know that this was not something she was proud of and she did not like me being a minister. She must have been hurt at some time and felt that people who tried to serve the Lord were hypocrites and she was very offended by them.

I was a minister and I could not stop doing what God had called me to do so it was very hard at their home. I had to get away privately to pray when she was not around. When I attended a service somewhere I could not talk about it when I got back. It was very hard for me to live there but I knew beyond a shadow of a doubt that God did not want me to leave. He had a reason and He kept revealing that to me. He was witnessing to my mother in ways I did not understand. It was very hard but I kept staying there doing the best I could believing that the Lord wanted me to be there. I was also witnessing to her husband at that time. He did not go to church and did not proclaim to have given his life to the Lord. I also witnessed to my sisters as much as I could.

I visited several churches while I was in that area. One day I came home from a church service where I had been asked to preach the message and my mother was waiting for me at the door and she was very angry.

"Mother, what is wrong?" I asked. "You and I are going to

have a talk," she said. She took me into the living room and we sat down to talk. "There is something you are going to have to understand. You are not going to keep preaching and doing what you are doing trying to be this way. This is just not what I think is best for you. This is not a good thing."

I could see that it was bringing conviction to her because of the bar she had and the way her life was. I didn't completely understand it, but she was very angry. She let me know that if I was going to continue to preach, I was not going to be able to live there.

I didn't know what to say, I had no other place to go at that time, I had very little money saved and I had no car. I didn't know what else to do but I could not deny my God and I could not deny that I was called to preach the gospel.

"Mother, I have to preach the gospel," I told her. "And I don't mean to offend or hurt you. I'm so sorry but that is something I have to do." She was so angry and bitter that she went in and began pulling my clothes out of the closet throwing them on the floor. It seemed Satan had really gotten in her and she said, "You are just going to have to get out and you are going to get out now! I don't care if you don't have anywhere to go! You can call somebody or do whatever you have to do! You have to go!"

I had no one to call and knew no one in that area other than some people I had met in a church. I didn't have any friends at all so I really didn't know what in the world to do but just go and see what God would do for me, I was very scared. That day was very cold and there was snow on the ground. It was thirty degrees or colder. All I had was a suitcase, a large blanket and my other clothes stuffed in there. The rest of my stuff was left at the house out on the porch.

I picked up the suitcase and blanket and started walking

down the road. It was very cold and I was so confused and hurt. I began to tell the Lord, "Lord, I don't understand! I just don't understand!"

I must have walked a good two miles and I am telling you I almost froze to death. I was so cold and there was no building I could get into where I could get warm. I had gone out to the highway so if someone would pick me up, I could go somewhere or ask for help but no one picked me up, not a soul and I was so cold I could hardly stand it.

I asked the Lord, "What in the world do you want me to do, Lord. Why have you put me in this situation?" I couldn't understand.

I looked down the road and saw a church quite a distance away. I was so cold I didn't know if I could make it that far or not. I finally got there and kept knocking until a gentleman opened the door. I asked him if I could come in because I was so cold. He invited me in and took me to a little room where he was staying. It was a small room in the church and he had a little heater, some blankets and he was sleeping there. I wondered what in the world he was doing here, no one else was in the church. He was a very nice man and I moved up close to the heater and wrapped some of his blankets around me. It was several hours before I felt warm again.

God did make a place for me to find, He did make a refuge for me. He did not let me die and I thank Him for that. Little did I know that God brought me here and He was about to do something incredible. I stayed all night in the church with that gentleman. This man had been accused of child abuse. Someone said he had beaten a child and sexually molested her but he said it was not true.

"Not a word of truth in it," he said. "But I can't stay with my wife and my kids now so the church is letting me stay here while the court is deciding what to do." He was so hurt and burdened and somehow I really believed him in my heart because of the way he talked. I believed that someone had falsely accused him and wondered why anyone would be so wicked and do that to this man.

I told him I was a minister and he must have wondered what I was doing in this kind of situation if God was really blessing me. I explained to him about coming from New York, my mother and all that had happened. Then he began to tell me he knew some people in churches where I could preach. We began to get close as we prayed together and I told him about Jesus. I asked him if he knew the Lord. He said he knew the Lord but he wasn't close to the Lord. He had never been real close to the Lord. I talked to him about things in the Bible that I had learned and explained to him how wonderful it is to be close to God. Here I am trying to witness to him and me not knowing what was going to happen to me or where I would be next. Little did I know that all the things I was saying to him were sinking in really deep.

I do want to say this, God did not let that seed go unwatered or not taken care of because I found out later he became a minister and was called to minister in nursing homes and churches. He worked with the very church we were in and he won many souls for the Kingdom of Heaven. I thought to myself that God even had a divine reason for that man to be there and for us to share the things that we shared. That was another reason for the situation I was in that I had not understand.

The next morning, being Sunday, the pastor came to the church. I had no way of taking a bath or anything so I was dirty and did not look very good for church. Everybody was coming in for church and I thought I needed to talk to the pastor and tell him I had stayed there the night before and everything. I pulled the pastor over and told him I needed to talk to him and he said we would talk after the service. When we talked after the service I told him about my situation, that I didn't have any place to go and I asked if I could stay there just a little longer. I wanted to stay a week or so until I could find a place. The other man was staying in the church so I asked if I could stay here with him.

What he said broke my heart and I really questioned if I should put this in my book. Then I decided I should put it in. People need to know how some people live sometimes, none of us are perfect. This minister turned to me and said, "Yes, you can stay at the church a week if you feel like it but you cannot use the heat in the church. You can't turn the heat on."

Isn't that something? He had a lot of members in that church that had plenty of money to keep us warm. That was why the man had the little heater in that room because they would not let him use the heat and this was in the middle of winter. "My God," I thought. "I can't believe what I am hearing." So I told the pastor, "Okay, I won't use your heat but I need a place to stay." That's when it dawned on me. I really believe what he was trying to do was put a little fear in me because he didn't want me to stay there thinking I would stay warm. I knew I didn't have anywhere else to go so I told him I would not use any heat and would stay in the room with the other gentleman.

He said that would be okay, I could do that for a week. He made it plain to me that I could only stay only one week. Since I could be in this church for only a week, I had to try to find some way to get around and find some help. I had no one to call, no money and no transportation, it was the middle of winter and I couldn't contact my sisters or any of the family because my mother and sisters were not very close and she told them not to help me. She had parted friends with me and this was the way it needed to be. My sisters never associated with my mother and did not go see her very much at all. They were not very pleased with the bar life that she lived.

I realized what I really needed to do more than anything was to go into the sanctuary and start praying asking God to help me. It was so cold in that church, sometimes it was hard to concentrate on praying. I would pray a while and then go in the little room and get warm and then go pray some more.

I told the Lord, "Whatever You have for me I will try to understand. Will You please send someone or make a way to get me a refuge? God, I am exhausted trying to come up with ways or what to do. I am turning it all over to You." I prayed and prayed until I was exhausted praying and nothing happened.

Then God decided to answer my prayer. I want you listen to this very carefully. I want you to realize without having any money, without having transportation, without a place to live in the middle of the winter, God heard my prayer. I never was so cold, so hungry and so confused in all of my life. They never brought us anything to eat but the other man had a friend, a lady who came by and brought him some sandwiches and things that he shared with me. That is literally what I ate.

Late one night I was praying at the altar and it was almost the end of the week, five days. I had really come to the end of myself and I have to admit, I thought I was going to die. I wasn't dying from not eating and being cold but from being depressed and hurt. I came to the place where I even began to question God. "God, I don't understand this one at all," I prayed. "I'm so cold and hungry and not one member of this church seems like they even care."

As I stayed in that situation, I prayed late that night until

I could pray no more. I am going to be honest, I gave up and thought whatever happens, happens. I thought I am not going back to my mother and be humiliated that way and she didn't want me there anyway. I just gave up. How many of you know that just about the time you start giving up is when God stands up? This was about to happen to me.

> *Even the youths shall faint and be weary, and the young men shall utterly fall: (31) but they that wait upon the Lord shall renew their strength; they shall mount up with wings as eagles; they shall run, and not be weary; and they shall walk, and not faint.*
> Isaiah 40:30-31

Chapter 19

THE DREAMER

And it shall come to pass in the last days, saith God, I will pour out of my Spirit upon all flesh: and your sons and your daughters shall prophesy, and your young men shall see visions, and your old men shall dream dreams.
Acts 2:17

I LOVE TO TELL THIS PART. The next morning I woke up and looked out the door of the church at the snow on the ground and it had gotten colder outside. I wondered if I should pick up the blanket with my things, put the suitcase in my hand and head out in the cold and take my chances. Would a car pick me up or should I wait until the next Sunday and beg for help? I was thinking to myself that I probably should just get my things, leave and take my chances. The man I had been sharing the room with was gone for the day. Some of his friends had picked him up so I was there by myself.

I heard a knock on the door so I went to the door wondering who it could be. There was an elderly man standing there. He had a hump on his back and looked as if he had some physical problems. He kept knocking and he had the biggest smile on his face. I opened the door and asked if I could help him. He just stood there very still and quietly looked at me.

He asked, "Is there a minister staying here at this church? Are you a minister? Do you preach?" "Yes sir," I answered. "I have preached many times." He looked at me and said, "Well, you are the one." "What do you mean?" I asked.

I have missed the last few services here because I've been sick," he said. "Last night I had a dream. In my dream the Lord revealed to me that a minister was staying in our church. He spoke to me specifically and told me to come to the church and said to ask for that minister and invite him to my home, talk to him and keep him for a while. I know it sounds crazy but that is what the Lord told me to do."

I couldn't believe this. Of course I went with this man called Woody who lived in a very old house with his wife and two daughters. He had Bibles everywhere and Christian books all over the house. I saw that he evidently loved God's word. We sat down and started talking about the things of God.

"I've been learning a lot of things in the Bible and here is something I want to show you," he said. He showed me many scriptures on fasting. We studied them; how it would break bondages and how it would cause a person's health to spring forth speedily. He was trusting it was going to happen for him and asked if I knew of these things. He asked if he learned to fast, would things happen, would healing be brought forth.

It was the most awesome study. He had done so much research. I wrote down many of these things and kept them and they dealt with my spirit. We were talking and he asked me where I would be working if I moved to this area. I explained the situation with my mother. He said he knew my mother and that she worked in the bar but he didn't associate with people like that.

"If your mother doesn't want you there, I don't blame you for not going back," he told me. He asked what I was going to do and I told him I had no idea what I was going to do next.

"I am going to pray with you," he said. "We will pray and God will do something for you. I want you to stay here until God does something. Don't worry, you will have something to eat. You don't need to worry. God is going to do something!"

It touched my heart. God had given a man a dream to make sure I would be taken care of. I could hardly sleep that night because I was thinking about what God had done.

The next morning we sat down to eat breakfast. "There is something I need to tell you," he said. "God spoke to me last night while I was praying. I questioned it and went around and around with it. I am convinced it is just the way it is. I prayed for the Lord to do something for you and He told me what I should do." "What did the Lord tell you to do?" I asked.

"The Lord told me to buy you a car," he said. This man did not have very much money, he probably was living on social security and his wife was in very bad health. He also had two daughters to take care of as neither one of them worked. I thought to myself, God I can't take something like this from this man.

"Sir, I'm sorry," I said. "You can't do this. In your situation, you can't do this." "Yes, I can," he replied. "Don't try to stop me because the Lord is telling me what to do."

He was a man on fire. This man told me we were going to go to the bank. He said he did not have the money but he was going to borrow enough money to get me a decent car so

I could get around. He said if I had a car I could go look for work. "Eventually," he said. "You will find a job and you will have a place to stay until you do."

I thought, he doesn't have money and this is going to put him in debt. I knew if this was what God wanted him to do I couldn't really say anything about it. I would let him do it but I would pay him back if this is what he wants to do.

We went to the bank in Palmyra, Indiana. I know all of this sounds strange but it is really true. He went to the bank and told the banker he wanted to borrow enough money to buy a car.

The banker asked him, "How much money do you need?" He told him about three thousand dollars to buy a cheap car to get around in. The banker asked him what he had for collateral since he didn't have much money in the bank and he was on social security. The man told the banker that he really didn't want the money for himself. He explained that he wanted to help me; that I was in a terrible situation, and I needed an automobile so he wanted the banker to give me a loan.

Of course the banker asked me where I worked and I told him I didn't have a job. He asked me where I lived and I told him I was living with Woody.

The banker looked at him and said, "I'm sorry, Woody. He is in a situation that we can't give him a loan. We just can't do this." Woody turned to the banker; I could see the fire in his eyes, he said "You listen to me, I have banked with you ever since I have lived in this town. I may not have a lot but what I have borrowed from you I have paid back. I do not owe anybody anything and I have just thought of something you can have for collateral, you can have my tractor."

The banker looked at him and told him the tractor was old but they could use it for some collateral. Woody looked at him and said, "You will either do it or I will take every penny I have out of this bank right now." The banker thought for a minute and said, "Okay, okay, we'll do it. We will hold your tractor for collateral."

Now Woody's tractor meant everything to him. He couldn't work anymore so he raised a garden and used his tractor for that. If they were to take his tractor away from him he would really be hurting. You know, it just kept eating at me, how in the world could this man do this? Then I realized I was experiencing the real love of God in an individual. God was showing me something about the love He puts in people's hearts. It goes beyond the way we love. The banker gave us the money and went home.

Woody said now that we had the money we needed to look for a car. He asked if I had any ideas about what kind of a car I wanted. We talked about it some and I told him what I might like. He told me we would not be able to be real choosy with the amount of money we had but he had a good friend who worked at a car lot. He would be able to help us get a good car. This was so wonderful the way Woody was helping me.

The next morning as we were sitting at the kitchen table, Woody asked me if I was ready to look for my car. I was ready and walked out the front door. There sat a car in the driveway.

"Whose car is that?" I asked Woody. "Is someone here?" Woody took a set of keys out of his pocket and held them up to me. He said, "Here, that's your car, I went early this morning and picked it up. You don't owe me, you don't have to pay me a dime. This is something I wanted to pay. This is what God told me to do."

"Oh, Woody," I said. "You don't know what this means to

me." I thought, now I have a way to get around and minister and I can go look for work.

He had given me a place to stay until I could do something. God, this is too good to be true.

The very next morning I started looking for work. The first thing I did was pull into the K-Mart parking lot in nearby Albany, Indiana and began to pray. "God," I prayed. "You show me where to go. Woody has been so kind and so good, please don't let him down. Let me find work so he will not have to continue to take care of me and I won't have to live under his roof. Please do something, Lord."

I drove on down the road and the first place I saw was a car auction place. I pulled over thinking I might go over and watch the auction but I really needed to go look for work. I got out and watched anyway. There were many people working there. Some of them were driving the cars through the auction and some were cleaning the building and doing other jobs.

I decided to ask for a job so I went to the manager's office. I told him I was new to the area and I was looking for work. I told him that I had worked at a hospital and he asked me what I had done and I told him I had been a janitor. He said they had janitors working there and he asked me several more questions. He said I seemed like a very nice man and he thought I would be capable of taking care of the responsibility of the building but what they really needed was a manager to be over the janitorial system. They didn't have somebody to oversee the janitors to get done what needed to be done in taking care of the building. He asked if I had ever thought about being a manager in an area like that. I told him yes, that I would love anything, it didn't matter what it was.

He immediately told me to come in first thing in the morning and I would be manager over his cleaning crew at the car auction and it was not a small place. There were quite a few people working there. I just couldn't believe it! I thought this was unbelievable and the pay he offered me was not bad. I couldn't wait to get home to tell Woody. When I told him he said, "See? God has blessed you and He is going to continue to bless you."

I began to work at the car auction and I met a lot of people who came there. I was able to walk around and talk to people, even witness to them about the Lord. They didn't mind my doing this and it was wonderful.

Soon I moved out of Woody's place and into an apartment by myself. I began looking for places to minister in the area. I had a job and a car and as I got paid I gave Woody some money until I had paid him in full for the car. I had to fight him to make him take it. He didn't really want me to give it to him but I wanted to give him back everything he had paid for that car.

God greatly blessed him for what he had given to me. God had already supernaturally given him back more money than he had borrowed. Money began to come to him through ways that hadn't even occurred to him, more than he needed to pay the loan back quickly. I can see why God did it because of the love for the Lord that Woody had in his heart. He got the money God sent him and he also got the money I gave him so he actually got paid back twice! He got enough to pay off the car loan and then he got that much again.

A person can never do wrong by trying to help and bless those people who love God and want to do what is right, especially those who are in great need. I learned something through this. I learned we really couldn't judge people because of the situation they are in. We really can't look at their character and think they wouldn't be in this situation if they were right with God. You never know what God may be doing. You never know where God may be putting them and why they are in the situation. It is our responsibility to do as Woody did and love each other and to give and help, and in doing that, God will multiply back to us more than we give.

> *But whoso hath this world's good, and seeth his brother have need, and shutteth up his bowels of compassion from him, how dwelleth the love of God in him?*
> 1 John 3:17

Chapter 20

THE REVIVAL THAT BROKE PHYSICAL AND SPIRITUAL DEFENSES

And were beyond measure astonished, saying, He hath done all things well: He maketh both the deaf to hear, and the dumb to speak.
Mark 7:37

AFTER I HAD MOVED into an apartment, I was looking for places to minister so I went to several churches talking to people. I visited a church out in the country near Corydon, Indiana. That church and two other churches came together to have a revival in a place called Buffalo Trace Park in Palmyra, Indiana. That was less than a half a mile or so to where my mother lived. The three churches were going to put up a huge tent for the revival. I came and visited that day and everyone was discussing the plans for the revival. They decided what they were going to do was have every minister who was there to come up, no matter where he preached. Of course I was a minister even though I didn't have a church at that time.

"We want the whole church to pray for these ministers

because we want to use these ministers in this tent revival," the pastor said. "We want to use the ones the Lord wants us to use, as our time at Buffalo Trace Park is limited to one week so we will only have five nights for our revival."

The churches were trying to determine which ministers God wanted to preach at this revival. The people began to pray and to lay hands on the ministers and the Spirit of God began to move. Then later they tried to decide who would preach. They chose two other ministers and they also chose me. I have no idea why but for some reason the people said they would like to hear me, since I was new in that area and they wanted to give me an opportunity to preach two nights.

"Wow, this is really wonderful," I thought. "Three churches in the area are coming together. I get to meet these people, I get to preach the gospel here, and try to win souls. This is wonderful."

Not a whole lot happened in the first two or three nights of the revival and I was to preach the last two nights. We had some great preaching but not many people had been saved. We were all getting really concerned.

The first night I preached from the Bible about Jacob; God had called him from a worm to be a prince. Jacob had been wicked but God changed him and caused him to have power with God. I talked about how wicked he had been and what God had done to change Jacob's life. The people really responded to the message as the Spirit moved among them. You know, my having been healed, I always mention the healing power of God. We decided to pray for people who needed to be healed physically as well as for people who needed to be saved. People came to the altar that night. They were being saved, being delivered and the power of God just really moved on them.

This may sound strange to some people but this is how the

Lord was moving. A young lady was sitting on the front row. I was still early in my ministry and so it was difficult for me to just walk up to someone and tell them I wanted to pray for their ears. It was hard for me to do at that time but I knew I had to obey God. So I asked the young lady sitting on the front row, "May I pray for your ears? The Lord wants me to pray for your ears." She looked at me and said, "There is nothing wrong with my ears."

"Could I have made a mistake here?" I thought. However, the Lord repeatedly impressed upon me to pray for her ears and I told her again that He wanted me to pray for her ears.

"Why in the world would the Lord want you to pray for my ears when there is nothing wrong with my ears?" she asked. I asked her if I could pray for her ears anyway and she said, "Yes, you can pray for my ears if you want to."

So she came and stood up front. I laid my hands on her ears and as I began to pray, God didn't have me pray to heal her ears, He just had me pray that He healed ears. I couldn't understand why God directed my prayer in that way.

I finished praying and she shook her head like it was kind of ridiculous and she went back and sat down. Everybody was looking at me rather strangely when all at once a lady all the way in the very back of the tent stood up and started coming down to the front. Tears were streaming down her face and she was carrying a little girl in her arms.

"Brother Connors," she said, coming up to me. "My little girl is deaf. She has been deaf since birth. I have been praying and doing everything I know to do. I can't stop believing. I have to hold on somehow. There has to be a way. I prayed for God to send me somewhere or show me how my daughter can get healed. Find a way please. When you started praying for that woman's ears, about how God can heal ears, I just knew that you were the one I needed to bring my little girl to. Would you please pray for her ears?" "Sure," I replied. "Sure I will."

When I laid my hands on that little girl's ears and began to pray I felt like fire was in my hands. I do not know any other way to explain it. I kept praying for her and all at once that little girl screamed. It scared some of the people and her mother jerked her back when she screamed that way. Instantly the little girl got quiet. You could have heard a pin drop in that place and I knew something had happened. I looked at the little girl and told her mother we needed to see if she could hear. I told the mother to turn her daughter facing the crowd. I snapped my hand to the right and the little girl turned her head. I snapped my hands to the left and she turned around to the left side. The little girl started mumbling sounds and her mother said she almost never made any sounds. I told the mother to walk away from me and I would make noises to see what she would do. I started making noises and the little girl was trying to make the noises I was making. That little girl could definitely hear.

When that happened the church broke loose in that tent. People started praising and worshiping and I mean it just broke loose. I knew this was a divine miracle from God. People began to tell others all over town. Some of the people had known this lady and knew that her daughter was deaf. They took her to the doctor and when he checked her ears he said she could hear. Someone put an article in the paper and everyone was talking about it all over town.

The next night I came to preach and it was the last night of the revival. I began to preach and to pray for people who were sick. Several people were saved. There was an elderly lady who could not bend up and down with her back and she was bent over. She was in very bad shape. We began to pray for her and lay hands on her and suddenly it seemed her back snapped and she stood up straight. She began to move around and walk back and forth. She began to kick and shouted, "I'm healed! I'm healed!"

Church broke out in that place again and people began to praise and to worship. Then I noticed in the very back of the tent there was a woman peeking around the side and looked at all the worshiping going on. It was my mother. My sister had brought her because they had heard about the little girl being healed. My mother wanted to come see what was going on. She was in the very back trying to hide and just listen to what I might have to say in these meetings. My mother knew the woman who had been bent over and was healed. She knew her very well and knew the condition she was in. My mother was confused and could not understand. She began to wonder if this could be real and didn't know what to think about it.

My mother was crippled in one leg. She had fluid built up in her knee and it was swollen so she had a limp when she walked and sometimes it was terrible. Her knee would swell up at least every other day and she would go to the doctor regularly to have the fluid drained but in a few days it would build up again. The doctors couldn't do much for her except give her medication. She couldn't walk very far without sitting down and my sister would have to help her to go places. My sister had helped her into the tent for the revival. But now my sister was helping her come up toward the front. "Oh, my God," I thought. "Lord, what are you about to do?"

I realized my mother was lost and maybe she was coming up to get saved. I prayed, "Oh, God. Please let this be." She wasn't coming to be saved. She was so amazed at the healing and she looked at me and said, "Glen, would you pray for my leg?" "Yes, Mom," I said. "I will pray for your leg."

I got down on my knees because I was so touched by the presence of the Lord, I couldn't help but cry. I looked at her and I laid my hands on her feet and I began to pray. Then I rose up and put my hand on the lower part of her leg and I began to pray. Then the Lord spoke to me. He told me to tell her to walk to the back of the tent and touch the tent pole and then come back up here. Let me tell you it was very hard to tell my mother something like that. Understand she didn't believe anything. She thought all this was fakery. For me to tell her to do something like that was hard but I just knew I had to obey God or I would have to live with that guilt.

I turned to my mother in front of that crowd and said, "Mother, the Lord spoke to me and told me to tell you to walk to that back tent pole and touch it and then come back here."

I will never forget what she said to me in front of that crowd. She looked at me and said, "You're crazy. You are crazy."

Suddenly when she said that, and I don't know why it happened, but people started praising and glorifying God. I saw my mother was realizing that God was involved in this. It didn't take a rocket scientist to figure it out the way the Spirit was moving. Everyone could feel the Lord moving. A sweep of the Holy Spirit was passing through the tent. My mother turned and kept looking at that tent pole while everybody was worshiping. She looked at it a good long time. She started toward the back of the tent. It was a huge tent and it was quite a way to walk to the back where the tent pole was.

My mother couldn't walk very far and my sister was helping her. "Don't help her," I told my sister. "Let her go. The Lord said for her to go there." "She'll fall," my sister said. "Let her go," I repeated.

My mother began to walk and she walked toward the tent post limping all the way. As she was going, the people kept praising and the praising got louder and louder. You would think she was going to fall the way she was having such trouble walking. She got to the back of the tent. Everyone was looking as if she was not going to make it. Then she touched the tent post.

She was still facing away from the crowd and we could not see her face. When she touched to post, she just stood there. She was not holding on to the post to hold herself up. She just stood there. Everybody wondered what she was doing. She turned around and had the biggest smile you can imagine on her face. She was moving her leg. She moved it up and down. She reached down with her hand and kept feeling of her knee.

"My God, my God!" she said. "My God, the swelling is gone from my knee. I have no pain. I can walk good." She walked perfectly all the way back to where I was standing. "The Lord has healed me," she said.

I thought to myself but I didn't say anything for a while. "Mom," I said. "You really need to get saved."

She was so excited about being healed she invited me to go home with her after the service. We sat up all night talking about the Bible. She had so many questions. We talked about the gifts of the Spirit. She wanted to know how this healing worked. How was it possible for the little girl who was deaf to hear and how was her leg healed? She told me she wanted to know about this. I told her as much as I could but she couldn't understand yet. She never knew the Bible or anything about God.

"Mom," I said. "You need to go to church and give your life to God." She never would give her life to Jesus even after He had done that wonderful miracle for her.

The revival was over and I went back to work. Mother would not hear spiritually. When I talked to her about her spirit she would not hear. She would not accept that. She did not want to hear that she needed to be saved. She rebelled against that. Once she saw that the little girl who was deaf and had never heard was healed supernaturally, she now realized that God was real but what was she going to do with this?

Then God opened her ears in a different way. One day while I was at work, my mother called and asked for me. She said, "Glen, I have something wonderful to tell you." I asked her what it was and she replied, "I knelt down in the living room by the couch and told the Lord I was sorry for every sin I had ever committed and asked Him to come into my life and my heart like you preached that night and said we should do. God gloriously saved me. He saved me. My life is different. I want to go to church with you and I want to learn about this God. Will you come home? Will you not work the rest of the day and just come home?"

My boss let me off work and I drove as fast as I could to her. I have never seen somebody changed so in all my life. My mother never said very many words without cussing. Now she was speaking with kindness and love, she never cursed. I'm telling you it happened instantly. She wanted to go to church.

"God has answered my prayers," I thought. "You know God, You are so wonderful. You helped me find my mother. It looked impossible. You not only saved her, You filled her with your love. How could I ever thank You?"

Then one day when I was at work, I got a phone call that said somebody was in the hospital and I was needed. I thought immediately it was my grandmother. My mother and her sisters had been taking turns taking care of her in their homes because she was bed fast. Everyone had been saying we needed to be good to Grandma because she was dying. I thought Grandma had passed away.

I got to the hospital and found all the members of my family in the chapel crying. I could see them through the window but I could not get in so I went to the desk and asked if they could let me in there. The lady at the desk asked if I was Glen Connors and I told her I was.

"They've all been waiting for you," she said. "Will you please come back here and identify the body? We need someone in the family to sign papers and such."

I was sure it was Grandmother who had passed away even though they did not say one word to me about who it was. We walked back there and when they pulled the curtain back I saw my mother lying there dead. They said they didn't know what happened to her but they had been told she got up from the kitchen table and walked to where my stepfather was and told him she thought she was going to pass out. She fell over and was dead instantly. They did not find a cause. It was not a heart attack. They didn't write down anything for the cause of her death.

That is when I realized that you do not have to be sick to die. All that has to happen for you to die, to leave this world, is for Jesus to call your name. When I saw my mother lying there dead, it was very hard. I had no idea that she had died. No one had told me, I just saw her. Having been a medic when I was in the service, I knew how to check to see if someone was dead. I checked her thyroid, I checked her wrist for her pulse and checked her airway. I checked everything. She was dead. I was so hurt I didn't really know what to do. I thought I was going to have an opportunity to be with her and now God had taken her to heaven. All I could think was that I had reached her in time. Now my mother has gone to be with Jesus. I know she is with the Lord. She gave me her testimony and she had let me know she had received the Lord as her Savior. It is a shame that she didn't get to go to church with me and we didn't get to do anything with the Lord together. The most important thing was she got saved and that one day we will be together forever. Thank God we will still be able to share our eternal lives together and not be separated forever. Praise God.

> *But I would not have you to be ignorant, brethren, concerning them which are asleep, that ye sorrow not, even as others which have no hope. (14) For if we believe that Jesus died and rose again, even so them also which sleep in Jesus will God bring with Him.*
> 1 Thessalonians 4:13-14

Chapter 21

THE MIRACLE MOVING HAND OF GOD

And a great multitude followed him, because they saw his miracles which he did on them that were diseased.
John 6:2

IN MY BOOK I wanted to have a chapter especially dedicated to God to tell you about some miracles that have taken place. I know I have already mentioned quite a few of them but I want to dedicate it to God Himself for being with me and doing everything He said He would do if I believed in Him.

I love the Lord with all my heart. I believe the Lord wants me to share some of the miracles I have seen in my ministry so that they will be left behind when I am gone. I believe it will be an encouragement for others who want to go into the ministry and do something for the Lord. I promise you that every word I am going to tell you about these events are true.

I would like to tell you about two people I thought were very special that I lead to the Lord. The first one is the one I shall never forget. It's about a young lady by the name of

Linda and her husband Gary. I was in Nashville, Tennessee at the time. I was playing country music and I've already told you about my life there when I was a writer for Casey and Elizabeth Anderson, Lynn Anderson's parents. While I was there in Nashville I also got a job working for an RV company where I cleaned the outside of RV's and such. While I was washing the outside of the RV's, Linda was cleaning the inside of them. I didn't know very much about Linda; she just came to work every day and cleaned the inside of the RV while I cleaned the outside. I had this long pole that I would wash them with. Each day we would talk a little bit during our lunch break. She never really talked a lot. One day I was singing a gospel song while I was working. While I was singing God touched my heart. He told me, "Stop washing and go in and tell Linda how you were saved. I want you to teach Linda the Ten Commandments."

I thought, "Oh, why would You want me to do that?" I thought maybe God wanted me to tell her how I got saved, maybe she needed to know that, but why would the Lord want me to teach her the Ten Commandments? Everybody has heard the Ten Commandments since they were children.

I tried to ignore it and kept washing. The more I washed the more troubled I got and I just couldn't do it anymore. The devil tried to tell me I shouldn't go in there and talk to her. I was supposed to stay outside. The devil told me I could get fired. I could lose my job. I wasn't supposed to go inside the RV. I washed some more and then I said, "Okay, Lord." I put down my sponge and went inside the RV.

"Linda," I said. "Come here. I want to talk to you a minute." When she walked up to me, I began to tell her how the Lord had saved me. You know I watched her while I told her my story and I could tell that she was not saved. Then I did what the Lord told me. I asked, "Linda, have you ever studied about the Ten Commandments?" "No," she answered.

"There is something I would like to do if you would like for me to," I said. "Let me teach you about them." I could tell she wanted to know about them. "I don't ever read the Bible or anything like that," she said. I told her about the first commandment. I told her that each day I was going to tell her the next commandment. She came to work the next day and while she was cleaning she came out and asked, "What is the next Commandment? What is the next one?" I told her the second one and then the third day she came back and asked what the third one was. I told her the third commandment the third day. Then I told her, "Linda, this is in Exodus, chapter twenty and you can read it for yourself and you can read the rest of the commandments. These are the commandments of God. This is the way God wants us to live and this is the way God really wants us to be. Wouldn't it be wonderful if we could all keep these Commandments?"

Linda went home that evening and opened up the Bible and began to read from Exodus chapter twenty. She read every one of the Ten Commandments. She came to work the day after she read these and I was working outside and I thought she looked sad. She was just so sad.

While I was working away, she came out and looked at me and said, "Glen, I read Exodus, chapter twenty about the Ten Commandments of God. I am so hurt."

I asked her why she was hurt and she wouldn't tell me why. That stayed on my mind and kept bothering me. I decided I would talk to her at lunchtime. Our foreman went out to lunch so Linda and I were working there alone. She was inside the RV and wouldn't come out to go inside the building for lunch because she was so sad. I knocked on the RV door and asked her if I could talk to her. She agreed and I went in and sat down and asked her what was wrong.

"Glen, when I read those Ten Commandments I realized something," she said. "I have broken every one of them. I could never really know God and God could never really love me." I almost broke. Then it hit my mind that she said she had broken every commandment. I didn't say it out loud but I thought, "You have committed murder?" I don't know why I thought that way unless the devil was trying to torment me. I just came out and asked her, "Linda, have you committed murder?"

"Yes," she said. "I have. One time I choked a woman to death. I was in a fight with her and I was on top and I put my hands on her throat. I choked her until she died."

She kept talking about all the other commandments and she had broken them. Then she started talking about her husband. "My husband sells drugs in our home," she said. "I don't smoke dope but I drink with them. I sit around with them. Our lives are so messed up and I am so confused. Glen, I have read these commandments and I have broken everyone of them. God could never love me, could He?"

I looked at her and said, "Linda, God loves you more than you could every think or imagine." "How could He love me?" she asked. "I have broken them all!"

I explained to her how God had died for her sins and He paid the price on the cross of Calvary because He knew that we needed to be forgiven for our sins. He paid for them all. There was no Commandment He would not be willing to forgive her for. When I talked to her and began to tell her about the plan of salvation, she just broke. She literally fell on her knees in the RV and began to cry. The tears were really falling.

"Why don't you and I pray because you can come to know Jesus?" I asked. "How can I?" she asked, still crying. I explained to her that she just needed to ask Jesus to come into her heart and life and ask Him to forgive her of her sins and realize what He had done for her.

"You need to believe that Jesus' blood can cleanse you from your sins," I told her. Then we began to pray. She kept praying and I knelt and prayed with her.

Suddenly she raised her head and looked at me and said, "Glen, I am saved! I know I'm saved! I'm saved!" She smiled and stood up and said, "God has forgiven me! I have held these things inside me all these years. I didn't think I could do anything because of the kind of person I was. God has forgiven me and I am saved!"

She was radically happy. After that happened she ran out of the RV and ran into where some of my friends who worked on the electrical part of the RV were working. She told them all about how the Lord had saved her. Of course they all looked at her as if she were crazy but she wanted to tell everybody.

"Glen, I can't wait to get home and tell my husband!" she said. I thought, "Oh Lord, he is a drug addict. What will he do to her? Will her life be in danger? What will happen?"

We were having a revival at church that week and I was preaching so she brought her husband one night. He didn't know where he was going. She got him in the car and brought him to the church. Since he was there he went in with her. When he came in and I started preaching the gospel, I watched him. I know he was remembering what his wife had told him. He began to see his life of sin and I saw him as he broke and this man did not walk to the altar, he ran to the altar. He prayed and called out to God and God gloriously saved him.

Today Linda and Gary are involved in a ministry. They go to church regularly and are serving God. Their home is drug free and they are witnessing for Jesus Christ. Isn't it wonderful that God can forgive us? He will even forgive someone who has broken every Commandment. I wanted to share that story with you.

There is another story about another person who was saved who has greatly touched me. It is about a man in New York. He was in a nursing home because he had a stroke. His sister was going to the church where I was going. She came to me and asked if I would go pray for her brother in the nursing home. She told me he was eighty years old and she knew he had never been saved. She didn't know if he had been to church. He had been around people who did not go to church. She was really concerned about him.

"My brother has been away from here most of my life and now he has come back here to live," she said. "I want somebody to talk to him about Jesus before he dies. Will you please do it, Brother Connors?"

I told her I would and we went to the nursing home. Her name was Dolly. When we got there and went to his room, I saw what the stroke had done to him. It was hard to look at him in that condition even though I had seen people in terrible conditions before. This man was all twisted, his mouth was twisted to one side and his hands were twisted and looked as if he was paralyzed on one side. The first thing I realized that he looked as if he was in another world and could not communicate. The first thing the devil talked to me about was that I could not talk to this man about the plan of salvation because he couldn't understand me. I really thought maybe I should leave. What could I say if he could not hear me or understand me? The Lord put a great impression on my heart. He reminded me how He never turned anyone away. Someone had come to me and asked me to do this and there was a soul in that twisted body. I was not to be concerned if he responded or if he did not. He could be responding even though I wouldn't know it. If I did not take responsibility and do what I was supposed to, that soul could go to hell. That really inspired me.

I bent over beside the bed and began to talk to him. I asked him," Sir, do you know Jesus Christ?" He didn't respond and I thought he was not able. Then his sister told me if I would take his hand, he would squeeze it sometimes if he wanted to say yes. I took his hand and bent over again and repeated, "Sir, do you know Jesus Christ and do you know that He died for your sins? Have you ever given your life to Jesus Christ?"

He never squeezed my hand. I didn't know how to take that or what that meant. "Can you nod your head or squeeze my hand to let me know?" I asked. "If you have not and you don't know Jesus as your Savior, would you squeeze my hand?"

This time he squeezed my hand. I felt it strongly. I bent over and spoke in his ear. "Sir, even though you might not be able to respond, I believe you can hear me because you squeezed my hand and that told me that you do not know Jesus as your Savior," I said. "I want to pray for you."

I told him the story of Jesus and all He did to forgive him and to save him and that Jesus could deliver his soul and if he were to die, he could live eternally with God. I told him I was going to pray and said, "You pray inside of yourself and ask the Lord to come into your heart to save you."

The Spirit of God really began to stir and move and Dolly was crying. Everyone in the room was crying because of the prayer I was praying. He made no response and you could not tell if he could even hear what I was saying. I ended the prayer and something began to happen. We looked at that gentleman and all at once a countenance come on that man's face and the twisted mouth and the twisted face began to straighten. It was moving slowly but it was straightening up. It happened right before my eyes and right before Dolly's and right before everyone in the room. We all saw it. As it was slowly changing and his face straightened up, the hand I was holding that was crippled began to straighten and he raised it up in the air.

"Praise the Lord!" he said. "I am saved! I am saved!" Everybody was absolutely amazed. He spoke with a voice as clear as you or I could ever say it. Everyone in the room could feel the presence of God in his voice and could see the gleam in his eye. Then immediately his face started to draw and his hand started to draw and went back into the state they were in. We were just overtaken. We knew nobody would ever believe us when we tried to tell what had happened. Dolly couldn't wait to get back to the church and tell her church family what had happened.

The next day her brother died in the nursing home. To me that was the most touching experience I have ever had with someone getting saved. Not only did the man get saved, and sometimes when we pray with someone to get saved, we cannot see what happens inside of him or her. But God gave real evidence to show to the people who did not believe, that this could be possible. This was a man who could not respond. He couldn't speak. We didn't know even if he understood. But yet, he did understand and God allowed him to let everybody know that he did and that praying with him helped him to get saved. He had called on Jesus inside himself. I just thought it was so wonderful.

I would like to tell you about another miracle that happened. I was attending a church in New York and met a woman named Eileen who was a member of that church. She was a very nice lady and she loved the Lord and attended church regularly. One day Eileen was on her way to church and something happened to her car and she slid off into a ditch and ran into a tree. When the car slammed into the tree the steering wheel jammed into her ribs and it ruptured her intestines. It did not puncture her abdomen but the force of the steering wheel ruptured her intestines. They rushed her to the hospital and she was bleeding profusely. One of the members of the church called me and said, "Eileen has had a wreck and she is calling for you. She is in the emergency room and she wants us to reach you."

I hurried to the hospital and the emergency room and told the nurse whom I was and asked if I could go in. She went in and checked and when they let me in I thought, "Well, this must be very serious because they always let me in but this time they had to check and see if it was ok for me to come into her room."

I went into her room and could not believe what I saw. There were two pans on each side of her and two nurses had two syringes and were putting blood into her. As fast as they put the blood into her, she was losing it. They were trying to keep the blood in her so she would not die. She was still able to respond and speak.

I walked over and laid my hand on her forehead and said, "Eileen, I'm here." "Glen, it's time to pray," she replied.

"Oh, my God!" I thought. "It doesn't look like this lady can ever make it." Suddenly something swelled up in me to take authority and to pray like I had been taught according to the word of God. I began to pray for her and I began to take authority and to call for Jesus to heal her. Jesus reminded me of a scripture in Ezekiel, chapter sixteen, verse six, that says "When I passed by thee and saw thee polluted in thine own blood, I said unto thee when thou was in thy blood, Live; yea, I said unto thee when thou was in thy blood, Live."

I began to pray and I didn't completely understand that scripture, but God was bringing that scripture to me to pray and I prayed it. Later on, I found out why God had given me that particular scripture. When I finished praying for her nothing happened. She was just like she was before and they were pumping blood into her as fast as they could. I stood there with my head hung down and I knew that I had done all I could. I was thinking I might never see Eileen again after that prayer just because I was looking at the result. I knew I prayed what God told me to pray.

I turned and began to walk out of the emergency room. Just as I opened the door I heard one of the nurses scream. Nurses don't get excited like that often. She said, "Eileen has quit bleeding! I can't believe it! She has quit bleeding!"

Then she told the other nurses to get the doctor immediately. It might be possible for them to do surgery on Eileen. The nurse took the pans and syringes out of the way in case the doctors could do surgery. There was no bleeding. The blood was not coming through the tube at all. The nurse just stood there in amazement.

The doctor came in and the nurse told him what happened and he said, "Let's take her to surgery because this might break through again and she could bleed to death." They cut Eileen open and they found a scar as long or longer than a finger where her intestine had been ruptured but something had caused it to seal up. The doctor said he could not understand it.

He explained it to me this way. "When I saw that scar on her intestines, I could see where it had bled and I could see where the blood was in her intestines but it was sealed," he said. "I thought maybe I should sew over it but I could not find any reason to do that. The way it was sealed, it couldn't bleed. I put one stitch toward the end of the scar but I realized there was no reason to do that because it was sealed up completely." The doctors cleansed everything and closed her up.

Eileen woke up after the surgery and was so happy and excited when the doctor said, "I don't understand it, but you are not bleeding. It has stopped completely. You can go home anytime you are ready."

Eileen came to church after her hospital stay and gave her testimony about how the Lord had healed her. It touched the hearts of the people in the church and stirred up things about healing so that people were coming to the altar every night to be prayed for to be healed and supernatural healings were taking place. I thought that was wonderful.

Another miracle happened while I was in New York. A lady called me one night and said, "I got your phone number from a friend of mine in the church. My friend said you pray for people who are sick. I am sick. Would you pray for me? Would you agree with me in prayer? I really need it."

I told her I would be glad to pray with her. She began by telling me that she had pneumonia and couldn't breathe well. She had an infection in her lungs and the doctor had given her antibiotics but she was worse and couldn't seem to get over it. She told me she was in a wheel chair. One leg was totally paralyzed. It had been that way for about eight years. She needed to get over the pneumonia and she really needed prayer.

We began to pray and take authority and to believe God and to come into agreement. Suddenly this lady began to shout. She began to praise the Lord and I heard a thump. "What was that?" I thought. She had dropped the phone. I could hear stomping noises. It was taking her so long to get back to the phone that I almost hung up. I sat there a couple minutes wondering what had happened. She was shouting so I knew the Lord had blessed her in some way.

She got back on the phone and told me, "Brother Connors, my leg, it's moving! My leg is moving normally! I got up and

I am walking and I am praising God! I am breathing right and my lungs are clear!" "Praise the Lord!" I said.

Later that woman came to church and told what happened to her. She was a young woman, and because of the things that had happened to her, several children in the church were touched by it and they gave their lives to Jesus Christ.

I would like to tell you one last event that took place. This was a very unique thing that happened to me and I can't tell you if this was an angel or not an angel. Many times I have wondered if it was. I had stayed home from work one day while I was ministering in New York. I was very tired and needed to stay home and get some rest. I got up early that morning and it was snowing very hard. I noticed that I needed a few things from the grocery store to cook a good meal. Where I lived was not far to the store and although it was snowing really hard, it was not very cold. I thought it would be fun to walk to the store and get the few things I needed rather than trying to drive in the snow.

I put on my big heavy coat and went outside. It was snowing so hard I could barely see. I walked out to the highway and a small car pulled over and stopped. A nice looking, clean-cut man that I thought was probably in his early thirties or forties was in the car. He looked at me and asked if I needed a ride.

"Yes," I replied. "I'm going to the store to get some food." He told me to get in and I did but he didn't start the car but started talking instead. He said, "There is something I have to give you."

"This man doesn't know me," I thought. "What does he mean he has something he has to give me?" He reached down under the seat of his car and handed me a little book. I thought maybe he was trying to get me to come to his church or was trying to witness to me. I put the book inside my coat and he looked at me and smiled. He started the car and drove only about a hundred feet and stopped. I asked what was wrong. "I'm sorry," he said. "But I have to turn around and go back the other way. I have to leave."

I told him that I was just going up to the store and could he take me there? He said, "No, I am going to have to leave. I'm sorry, but I have to leave. Then he looked at me and said, "We'll meet again. We will meet again."

I thought that was very strange, but I opened the car and got out. He turned around and went the other way. I went on to the store and bought my groceries.

When I got home I opened my coat and took out the little book the man had given me. In front of the book was some kind of printing by hand. The inside pages looked like it might have been done by a computer although it was really hard to tell. The book was about numbers in the Bible. It began to explain the meaning of numbers in the Bible and why these numbers had these meanings. I had never seen these numbers and it amazed me. It was telling me about the stars in the Bible. There were prophecies in the stars and these numbers had something to do with these. It just blew me away.

I took the book to several people and asked if they had ever seen anything like that and no one had. I took it to the library and they had never seen anything like it. I wondered where this book had come from. At that time in the church I had been teaching about the stars. I was also studying the zodiac signs and how those signs represent and glorify God instead of the way astrologers have used them to read people's futures. That is not the will of God. I was showing that this thing had a real purpose and that these constellations and stars had a prophecy about Christ.

Then one night I went to sleep and I dreamed. In this dream

God spoke to me and told me to count the numbers of those stars in those constellations of the prophecies of Christ. He said, "Find the meaning of those numbers and you will find the meaning of those prophecies." It blew me away. I was consumed with it and I went to the library. I tried to find exactly how many stars were in each of the constellations according to what the scientists have seen. There are the stars we can see and there are stars we cannot see. I got the number of the stars in each constellation and then when I had this book it explained to me what the numbers mean. I took the number of the stars and wrote what these numbers meant and it explained the prophecy of Christ in each one. God wanted me to have that so I could teach on that and prove to people that these stars are not for our lives to be predicted and not for our future to be predicted by the stars. The Bible says, "The heavens declare His glory." These constellations that circle the earth are prophecies about Christ that will come to pass on this earth until the Lord will return and rule and reign over eternity and He will set up His kingdom.

I don't know if that man was an angel. I know that God got that information to me just when I needed it to be able to convince those people in New York who were caught up in astrology and in all those different things to break that bondage that was in their life. They needed to see the true purpose for the stars.

I still have that book. Once in a while I open it and read it. The book doesn't have many pages but there is so much wisdom in those few pages that you could study for years and not get all the knowledge that is behind all the things written in that book. I know that God gave that book to me to show me some special things that I would never learned if I did not have it.

If that man was an angel, I know that one day I will see him again.

Be not forgetful to entertain strangers; for thereby some have entertained angels unawares.
Hebrews 13:2

Chapter 22

THE GIFT OF CONTENTMENT TO MY LIFE, MY WIFE

And the rib, which the Lord God had taken from man, made He a woman, and brought her unto the man. (23) And Adam said, This is new bone of my bones, and flesh of my flesh: she shall be called Woman, because she was taken out of Man. (24) Therefore shall a man leave his father and his mother, and shall cleave unto his wife: and they shall be one flesh.
Genesis 2:22-24

THIS MEANS SO MUCH to me that it is hard to put into words and I really want to say this right so I guess I will start this way. Being married before, I feel it's best not to talk about the bad experiences I have had and all the hurtful feelings involved. I would rather talk about the blessings from heaven that have come from the marriage that has lasted and how beautiful it is. My wonderful wife fills my life with so much contentment, even today.

Her name is Edna and I love her so. I met this young lady when she started coming to the first church where I was a pastor.

Our desire was to live for Jesus and we wanted a home where we could glorify the Lord. God has joined us together in marriage and we have been through a lot of trials and tests. I am going to tell you it hasn't been easy. If anybody tells you that his or her marriage is easy I would really question it. When you want to do a work for God, and try to have a Godly home, the devil is going to do everything he can to try to destroy those things because that is such a treasure to the Lord. The Lord would love for us to have a Christian home and to be that example and to have a place where people can come and know about Him. That is the way He wants our lives to be. The Lord desires us to have a place of shelter and love.

I would like to say this about my wife. My wife may not be a very big woman in stature but she is big in a lot of ways. She is a small lady but she is strong because of her faith. Sometimes when I get to the point that I think I would like to throw up my hands and quit, and, oh yes, I get like that just like everyone else in the world does, my wife always seems to find some way to encourage and help me. She shows me that I need to continue to have faith in God because God can always work things out.

Yes, she goes through trials like I do and I have to help and encourage her and lift her up. The Bible says that if a man has found a wife he has found a good thing. I know what that means now. I had to go through a lot of hurts and trials and lots of things for that to happen in my life. I would like to say to every man reading this book: if you do not have a wife you might think that your life is blessed and you can go out and live and do whatever you want to do to have a good time because you are single and free.

Take some advice from someone who has experienced it. Having a good wife to come home to who cares about you and loves you, one who stands by you and understands you, is a much better life. You see, the carefree life is just there for a while and you have to go out looking for it again. It only lasts for a moment but a commitment with someone, especially with Jesus Christ in it, can be one that can be wonderful and can be forever. I believe with all my heart that this commitment that I have made with my wife is wonderful and one that I am going to keep until the day I die. I love her with all my heart and she has been everything to me. She has helped me do what the Lord would have me do even when I didn't have money or support from other people, even when people thought she shouldn't support and help me.

I would just like to say, "Thank you, Edna," in this book. I would like everybody who is reading this book to know that she has been the contentment of my life in this world. In spiritual matters God is always my contentment but in this earthly world my wife has become my contentment. She has been my comfort and I believe she is what the Lord wants a wife to be.

I would like to say this. I do not know where the Lord is taking me next but after everything that I have been through and everything God has brought me through, God has finally given me a home. You know that home is not the house that I live in.

That home is from that commitment that my wife and I made together and I now feel like I have a place where I belong. I am so thankful that God has brought me through all that He has brought me through and I am still able to glorify Him and praise Him.

For of Him, and through Him, and to Him, are all things: to whom be glory forever. Amen.
Romans 11:36

EPILOGUE

MY FINAL HOME

I WROTE THIS BOOK because I wanted to able to leave something behind that somebody else might see and know that God is truly God. If they will learn to put their trust in Him maybe they will not have to go through some of the hard things that I have had to go through. I give praise to God for everything He has done for me and I give Him all of the glory forever and forever. My prayer for you who have read this book is that you would make up your mind and get it settled that you are going to serve God. I pray that you may experience some of the blessings I have experienced, have the opportunity to do greater things for the Lord and that you may know what it feels like to go from glory to glory. I hope that if you have read this book and never meet me, that we will meet in the kingdom of heaven, be able to sit down and talk and you will be able to tell me about the things God has done for you.

Think about it. Time will be of no necessity and we will be able to enjoy it all through eternity. **Isn't God wonderful?**

The Lord bless thee, and keep thee: (25) the Lord make His face shine upon thee, and be gracious unto thee. (26) The Lord lift up His countenance upon thee, and give thee peace.
Numbers 6:24-26

—Glen Connors

To purchase my books, CD's or Soundtracks please call me at 765-349-5545.

You can sample my songs on any site that sells music or YouTube. Feel free to send comments to my e-mail address wer4him@att.net.

May God Richly Bless You,

Glen Connors

www.ingramcontent.com/pod-product-compliance
Lightning Source LLC
Chambersburg PA
CBHW030152100526
44592CB00009B/234